The Portraits of Desired Minds

By Shawn Ruter

Covers Ill. by Ashley Naus

Magic Circle Productions

Acknowledgements

Thanks go to Mom and Pop for their years of support as well as our wacky interactions which surely led to my inspired, incoherent ramblings. On second thought, maybe I should retract that thanks.

Ashley Naus too gets my mention, for without her continued backing when the stories and times were the roughest, I may never have finished putting pen to paper. Also for the beautiful cover designs you *arteest*.

And naturally I shan't forget my two close pals Jeremy and Steve who I trash-talked before glorious battle during much needed rest.

Lastly, many thanks go out to the cosmic energies that reverberate about our beings and alter the microcosmic fabrics in such a minute way as to influence or suppress action in almost unnoticeable ways. So does the butterfly flap its wings…

Contents

The Portraits of Desired Minds

Beware Itsy Bitsy

"Aaah!" The lady screamed. She had just encountered the horrific result of that mad scientist's efforts. No longer only man, numerous hairy legs dangled, twitching feverously. He approached slowly, and with a click it all vanished.

Charles Badwick sat in his comfy reclining leather chair in darkness for a while contemplating why he always did this to himself. Horror movies always scared him, but he loved the ideas behind the plot involved. He had seen many, but usually missed the ending because he always ended up too emotionally involved. So there he sat in his chair, in front of a darkened screen, tired, with the acknowledgment of having wasted his time once more. With a sigh Charles Badwick attempted to shake off his chills and retire to bed.

As he climbed the stairs in darkness alone, he thought about the movie. Good idea for a film, "Beware Itsy Bitsy." Another story about testing on nature, like storms, or in this case, spiders, gone wrong. Charles had thought himself a fool around halfway up, after all, he hated spiders. They were, well, he just thought they were gross, no matter how helpful in the big sense. Plus, they always made him feel crawly. At the top of the stairs Charles turned toward the bathroom for the usual pre-bed rituals, where he flicked on the light after grabbing his toothbrush.

"Aaah!" Charles screamed. A strange-looking spider dangling from its own thread hung directly before his face. In a gut reaction Charles swatted the spider, where it flew to the ground. He raised his foot viciously as the arachnid staggered disoriented. Down his foot went again. Charles regained composure before seeing what remained from the actions of shock.

He raised his foot and expected there to lay a fresh corpse, but there was no trace of the damned thing. No legs, nothing. Not on the floor, not on the bottom of his shoe, not under the sink, door, or anywhere Charles checked meticulously. He felt all crawly again.

"Just my luck. Can't watch a horror movie, can't fix my car, can't even keep calm enough to kill a stupid spider. Yep, great timing. Geez. I hate spiders." Charles shook his head, feeling ashamed of his masculinity. He decided to forget the whole thing as he crawled into bed.

Things weren't so easy for Charles. That was the problem with him and horror movies: nightmares. He dreamt he was in the movie he watched, in the role of a victim. Right as he was about to be captured by the mad scientist's mandibles, he woke up in a sweat.

Charles looked at his clock. "Almost two. Almost two A.M.," he sighed. "Work is going to be a pain tomorrow."

Charles Badwick got up from bed and proceeded to the bathroom to clean away the chilled sweat that made clothes stick to his body. Charles felt that gross wet slide as he flicked the light on again.

"Aaah!" Charles yelped. He stepped backward carelessly and almost tripped against the wall. "Not again!" Charles knew it was spring, the time when *they* started coming back, but why twice in one night? He rose up angrily from the whole mixture of the night and punched the mirror. He crushed the spider that dared to approach him again, a little too hard. He had accidentally cracked his mirror, and apparently his hand, or so he judged by the blood that dripped from it. He had little time to tend to the wound though, because he got that crawly sensation again, but it felt so much stronger. Charles quickly brushed all over his body and didn't want to believe what he felt. He darted his eyes to two, maybe three other spiders staggering about, after which began to flee.

With more agitation Charles crushed one more under his bare foot. Another spider seemed to escape into the darkness beyond the bathroom, but the last one skittered into the closet. Charles dug and threw various items from the closet, but he couldn't find his enemy.

"That's it, I'm tired of this. Really tired. It's over, now." Charles stated this knowing full well he needed more sleep. But he also knew he wouldn't be able to sleep with such a tingling shudder running over his body. The bastards were crawling on him! Charles begrudgingly tromped downstairs, grabbed his keys, and proceeded to drive his 2004 Aveo to the local 24-hour Convenie-mart.

He should have bought that insect spray when it was on sale at the grocery store, maybe he shouldn't have watched the movie. Why didn't he get the house fumigated a year or two ago when he had that ant problem? So many superfluous thoughts raced about his head. It didn't matter anyway, he was at the Convenie-mart, he'd exchange the pointless small talk to barter the necessary poisons tailored by some grand alchemist to fell the intruders in his home. He raised the spray-container high above himself triumphantly, as though a trophy, almost leaping into his Aveo with anticipation. He turned the key, the sounds of the engine crank up, when after moments Charles noticed it didn't seem to turnover.

"Oh You've got to be kidding me!" Charles lowered his head slowly onto his steering wheel. Any high left from getting his new weapon were quickly silenced by Charles' seemingly poor hand in life. Badwick, Badluck, it didn't seem to matter how you pronounced his last name.

Charles attempted to look under his hood, but knowing so little about cars he couldn't pop it. So Charles began his walk home. Luckily the local Convenie-mart really was local, a mere five blocks. He began to wonder why he didn't pay the extra money for whatever that mechanic spoke of last time he got his car serviced. But mostly he was trying to occupy his mind.

Charles lived in a nice neighborhood, but there weren't many street lights, and his circumstances only made everything stick out like a poorly painted house. Twigs cracking sounded like a sonic boom, rustling leaves an airplane engine, and tiny spider webs on street signs turned from invisible to terrible eye sores. Then again, spider webs were a path Charles' mind probably shouldn't have went down, for his mind was stuck, the paranoia filling the air.

Too well he became conscious of his nightmare. Dark hallways, dark streets, same concept. He was being watched or followed, from the ground or trees, or, or... It almost seemed a good idea to turn back, but he was already closer to home than the other options. After all, it was *his* home. The boys at the office would laugh at him for having ran from his house because of some household spiders. Despite that, Charles grasped the spray-container tightly against his chest with an alert-outlook.

By the time Charles reached home, he regreted the entire venture. He stepped into a greater darkness than that outside and had trouble adjusting to the light conditions. He stepped forward cautiously when something brushed his face. Charles panicked and flailed his arms about, swiping away. He heard a thump on the carpeted ground beside him. Squinting downward he noticed he dropped the spray-container, and the capped appeared missing, likely forced off from the drop. Feeling outward, Charles filled with chagrin when it turned out to be the drapes. He reached for the spray-container and grasped it firmly in hand. It had a somewhat sticky touch, but Charles chalked it up to the can accidentally firing off somewhere between descent and impact with the ground.

Back to his normal, albeit tired, self, Charles Badwick walked upstairs. Upon touching the railing, he noticed it was also sticky, which he assumed was a consequence of having picked up the spray-container a moment earlier. At the top of the stairs, Charles made a beeline to the bathroom. Something else swiped his face. He wiped away again, but the substance was stickier, adhering powerfully to skin and hair.

He tried to flick on the light switch, but was met with arduous effort, because the switch too was covered in this gross, tacky substance. After several attempts, Charles cranked the lights on. Moving ahead, adjusting to the intense change in contrast, his hand laid to rest on the side of the bathroom door. He reached for the frame adjacent, only to be met with a thick stringy object. He witnessed a terrible sight. A cobweb! This sticky, white stuff was everywhere. It covered the walls and ceiling, and many strands led to the floor, forming a beautifully hideous gargantuan spider's web.

Charles didn't have time to admire the craftsmanship. His eyes darted about and heart rate soared, he saw innumerable groups of small eight-legged nightmares surprised at the appearance of Charles as Charles was the countless spiders. Several moments fluttered before either side reacted. With sudden intent, the spiders advanced. Charles was terrified as some spiders let out tiny screeches to match their malicious skittering.

Turning to run, Charles' fight-or-flight mechanism set in a harrowing tunnel vision focused on getting downstairs. Nearly as many spiders had sectioned off the exit to the stairs, newly formed webs ordaining the upper section of the hall. Charles became entangled in the webs. He used his new weapon, the last beacon of hope. Or at least Charles Badwick tried. A spray shot into the air, directly upward, most of the fluid covering his index finger. Charles glanced and witnessed what he feared. There was no spray nozzle for the damned thing!

"Agh!" Charles profusely sweated. "A defective can! Or, no, no way…"

Charles thought this was all some terrible nightmare, organized spider marches. And… But they couldn't have possibly had the intelligence to dismantle an aluminum spray-container.

There were so many legions he could have sworn he almost saw the light reflected off their opal eye sets, feel their hairy legs brushed against his, their wretched fangs dripping with any amount of poison. Charles could only do what was left to him, flailing. He tried so hard to crush the spiders as they approached, but only succeeded in killing off a very small number, a pittance to the masses. His heart pounded almost to the point of giving out, especially when that intense crawly feeling came. Charles inadvertently jumped over the main force, unfortunately back toward the bathroom. Sensing a chance, he rushed to the bedroom, adjacent to his current location. It was sealed shut with webbing. Panicking force released the seal.

What Charles witnessed almost caused the contents of his stomach to expunge. The bedroom was covered, like new wallpaper or carpeting, in a fine layer of skittering tiny monsters. Charles queasily turned, blood from a rapid heartbeat darkening vision, when the last straw finally came. A large arachnid hung from a thread, meeting eye-to-eye. He blew out like a candle.

Darkness gave into light when Charles Badwick awakened. Every hair follicle seemed to perk up when he remembered what happened. Charles glanced briefly to see he was alone, laying on his bed. Charles smiled broadly, sweat droplets quickly cooled, and he felt at ease. Looking up with a relaxed tone he realized it was all one big stupid dream.

"Geez, I hate those dumb horror movies. They *always* get the best of me." Charles chuckled somewhat.

Charles tried to stretch, when he realized he couldn't. He was bound fast. He raised his head to look down at himself. He was lying on his bed covered in a sticky, stringy, white substance, immobile. Just then Charles remembered his bedroom ceiling wasn't painted with an artistic brown and black speckling.

The ceiling seemed alive as it shuffled, the spiders adjusted themselves, some switched positions, others dropped down on their thread to get a better look at their prey.

"I see you are awake," a booming voice spoke with a somewhat domineering tone.

Charles turned to see the large arachnid witnessed before passing out. A very ornate spider. Its back seemed professionally painted with a red hourglass, numerous patches of thread strewn about the hair on its body. If Charles hadn't known any better, he would have said the thread almost looked like royal clothing. Beside this large spider stood another spider, roughly half the big one's size. Up close Charles could see a very faint red hourglass on this one too. It seemed very unnerving to Charles this spider looked familiar. Of course, it was more unnerving that the voice he heard came from a spider.

"You think you're pretty tough don't you Mr. Badwick? You think that just because you have height and girth you control the world." Said the large spider.

"W-What are you talking about?" Questioned Charles, trying not to pass out again. "Literally, how are you able to talk about this? You're a spider!"

"Oi! He thinks we be dumb just because we don't yammer on foul, pointless speeches." A voice yelled out. In short order two brown recluses crawled over to the hourglass-backed spiders. One of the two bowed. "Oh sorry *me lord*, I didn't realize we should take a break from work to stop for idle chit-chat."

Charles couldn't believe it. Not only could spiders talk, but they were also capable of biting sarcasm.

"Calm yourself BR1. I employed you and BR2 to watch over my son, while I," The big spider rose two of its legs as it began, "The King of Spiders, attended my royal duties. I guess you were not even capable of something so simple."

"Ey, Apologies me highness, but the lad, me and BR2 started on about the recent food shortage when we looks back and find the lad missin'! We looked high and low, but I tell you he's stealthier than a boll weevil!"

"Got that right mate. I were there, I can verify. Quite skilled your young lad." BR2 said as he backed up his comrade. Charles guessed they must have been guards. They sounded almost the same too, so it was hard to tell either apart.

"And I was just going off for a bite to eat when that brute attacked me!" Yelled back the smaller spider standing next to the king of spiders.

"Which brings me back to our main point," Interrupted the King of Spiders. "You tried to murder *my* son in cold blood. My flesh and blood. My only rightful heir left, and you tried to rob him from not only me, but future generations to come." The King of Spiders started to become increasingly agitated as he recited this speech, "Do you realize the penalty for attempted murder on a member of the royal court?"

There was a very long and uncomfortable pause that followed. Charles felt all the sets of eyes fixed on him. He realized shortly that the Spider King was waiting for an answer. Charles attempted to lighten the situation by noting that spiders may understand the intricate concept behind sarcasm, but they didn't appear to grasp rhetorical questions.

"Uh," Charles paused, "I don't know."

"The penalty is death!" King of Spiders rose his legs triumphantly. The legions of spiders cheered. It was hard to pick out the dialects, but it sounded an awful lot like a high-pitched call for blood. The ceiling looked like it was slowly collapsing.

"I didn't do it! I swear I'm innocent!" Screamed Charles. A motion from the King of Spiders stopped the descent.

"Explain yourself," demanded the King of Spiders.

"I wouldn't harm your lad, I'm a very passive guy. Plus your son seems like a class act." Charles figured lying was worth a try. The King of Spiders did not seem pleased. He began to pace back and forth across the nightstand.

"You expect me to believe that you're a peaceful man, yet tonight many children must begin growing up without their fathers, some completely orphaned. All because of your intent to remove us from our home!" The King of Spiders was a spider, but he sure presented inspiring speeches. Soon Charles could hear slight whimpers and cries in the distance.

"But you were destroying my house!" Charles said this with little thought, but in retrospect if he was going to be killed, he may as well have made his point.

"Need I remind you that this wooden structure was once absent, and we lived a lucrative life on the plains that resided before?" The King of Spiders shot back. "We could have moved, sure. We could have packed up our bags and headed westward, leaving behind everything we knew. But we didn't. We made a stand. We even stayed politely out of your way. But you had to get involved in our politics. Then it got personal.

First you tried to kill my son, Itsy Bitsy. When we wanted to talk on our own turf, which we were in the process of creating, you go and smash our valuable architecture and slay our noble men and women." Cheers from the crowd for blood cried out once more. "And don't pretend you weren't planning all this." Somehow the King of Spiders made a snapping sound with his legs. This appeared to cue BR2 to drag something over. It was the spray nozzle. Charles was dumbfounded. They had thought of everything.

"But..." Charles had fallen short on words. He was always terrible in debates, but something more pertinent entered his mind. Had he actually tried to kill the King of Spider's son? Like a candle ignited, Charles' mind fired up. "Wait, your son, Itsy Bitsy. That's him? I recognize you!"

"Oh! As good as a confession me thinks highness. Just give the word sir and I'll pump him brim-full o' venom." BR1 made haste toward Charles' person. Charles tried to struggle away, but the sticky webbing held him secured. In a moment's notice he felt a small tingling sensation on his forehead. Charles tried not to picture the thick furry legs swaying on his face.

"Wait, wait!" Charles picked up the slack. "What I mean is I was set up. It's true! He snuck up on me. I'll admit, I uh... I acted without thinking and... And that wasn't right of me. But I was startled. Flicked on a light, Itsy Bitsy, a fine boy, right in my face. Okay, I've killed a spider in my time, even torn down a few webs..."

"Oi! That were you? All this time I be thinkin' it were me ex-friend Doddi Loongleg being jealous of me fine web-crafting, stealing away me meals. And it turn out to be you?" BR1 interrupted. "I'm sorry Doddi ol' pal!"

"It's alright!" A faint voice in the crowd yelled back.

"And I'm really sorry about that BR2," Charles apologized.

"Oooi! I'm BR1, not BR2! *He's* BR2," BR1 nodded toward BR2. Charles could feel BR1's twitched touch as he positioned himself toward the crowd. "He be thinkin' we all look alike! We just another tally for his murderous rampage!"

"Yeah, he tried to kill me," Itsy Bitsy concurred. More yammering from the crowd spurred, and Charles had to think fast if he was going to save himself from the oncoming mob.

"Hear me out! Okay, I did some bad things, I'll be the first to admit, but I stand by what I said. You're no better." What Charles said only seemed to confuse the crowd. Still, he continued, "Are not all of us, every one of us, guilty of the same crimes? Are any of you seriously suggesting you haven't accidentally caused the death of something smaller than you? You with your web traps? Is this what your parents and friends in the afterlife, or whatever you spiders believe, would have wanted? For you to become the giant you all seem to hate? I'm a normal guy who got scared in the normal way, and in the end, aren't we all just a little scared in this big cruel world?"

There was nothing but silence for what must have been a minute. Charles almost lost his composure, when he heard whimpers, slight cries, and whispered agreements slowly growing throughout the crowd. Truly Charles had touched them in some sort of special spider way. The loudest of the tear-filled legions had been, ironically, BR1.

"Oi. Oi. Had you all wrong mate," Sniffled BR1.

"Hey now, I think you're all forgetting he tried to kill me!" Shouted Itsy Bitsy.

"Itsy Bitsy, Mr. Badwick mentioned you set him up," Interrupted the King of Spiders. "You weren't lying to me about sitting in the corner minding your own business were you?"

"Hiding in the corner?" Charles scoffed, "He was dangling in front of my face when the lights came on."

"Itsy Bitsy," The King of Spiders grew more suspicious. "Why lie about your whereabouts?"

Itsy Bitsy seemed to squirm and fidget, adjusting to one leg, then the other, then the other, then the other. "Alright, I'll admit it! I saw the poor sap freaking out to some lame picture images. Figured I'd give him a quick scare and be on my way. So I hid in the bathroom, right next to the mirror where I could check out my hamstrings while I waited. I never would have expected he was going to kill me for having fun with a little prank! I almost didn't escape with my life, much less intact. I still feel sore in my lower legs. I can only thank the great priestess Arachnia that I was narrowly spared, crawling away into a small crack in the closet. But I'm still the victim here! He'd have killed me, you, anybody; given the chance. He's only acting nice now because we were about to execute him."

Charles knew this was true, but the spiders didn't have to know about the eventual call to the exterminators, if he made it out of the webbing alive. The King of Spiders paced again. He did this for some time, and looked lost in thought.

"Hmm... It appears I owe you an apology of sorts Mr. Badwick. I had no idea the deliberate intentions of my son's efforts. To think, a lad next in line acting so... So unkingly. Well, I assure you, though it pains me to say, Itsy Bitsy shall be punished." The King of Spiders said this with another snapping sound, which was a signal for BR2 to escort Itsy Bitsy away.

"I'll be back Badwick, mark my words!" Itsy Bitsy screamed as he was being drug away.

"A couple runs through the water spout ought to teach him a lesson in responsibility," The King of Spiders said to himself assuredly. He turned a sad tone, "I haven't felt this betrayed since my wife and I consummated our relationship. She tried to eat me!"

"Well, I guess that makes it a night then, you guys can loosen this webbing, and bygones will be bygones," Charles suggested cheerily to the King of Spiders' rather personal conflicts.

"Not so fast, Mr. Badwick. We've still some things to resolve. We may have deduced the ploy set by my son, but you still shouldn't have tried to kill a king's son. I think the purchase of your poison is proof enough your contempt for us. Still, I am a fair king, so I present a proposition. We can live in harmony, together, or my personal guard, BR1 can give your nervous system a taste of our own specially designed poison. I also remind you once again that we *are* in a food shortage. We've eyes everywhere, so don't even think about betraying us to delay for outside help."

A quick decision. "Well, guess I don't have much choice."

"Then we have an agreement. Another strand to the web!"

There was a sudden rapid shifting of the ceiling as the king's mantra was shouted over and over again by cheering spiders. Some, however, got too excited, when BR1 accidentally bit Charles. The pain was intense, and some of the spiders rushed over.

"Oh poppycock." The last thing Charles heard from BR1 before he passed out.

Charles awakened several hours later, very groggy and sore. He felt a sense of disorientation rush through his body. He was almost too sickened to get out of bed, a hassle anyway from the combination of loose webbing and sweat that covered his body. He pealed himself from bed into a pounding headache. He tottered into the bathroom with clouded vision.

In the mirror he saw an intricately woven sign that read "Welcome to the family." Through the spaces in the sticky, white webbing he examined his forehead. A large bump presented where that dumb brown recluse accidentally bit him. The bump created colors of purple, black, and blue splattered about the wound. With a begrudged sigh he walked cautiously downstairs to find something to soothe his aching mind. Charles Badwick was definitely calling into work.

Charles stepped into his kitchen with a fresh view on things. He noticed most of the mess upstairs was gone, and there was little activity from afar. Up close, however, he noticed spiders crawling across his counter, carrying sacks of sugar cubes and other various items. Charles turned on the coffee pot and opened a cupboard to grab his coffee mug. He almost poured coffee into it, a mistake considering the egg sacks inside. After he grabbed a fresh mug, cleaned thoroughly, he poured himself the best part of waking up.

The flavor a headache's panacea. No creamer today, Charles was going black. It fit in well with his outlook of the new living arrangements. One spider crawled over and explained his head wound was quickly treated with a anti-venom, so he didn't have to worry about impending death, but Charles Badwick didn't care to listen. He just wanted to sit and read his newspaper, which was conveniently laid out for him.

Charles noted the generous favor. He could get used to perks like that. After all, he got over arachniphobia in one night. Charles tried to sit down at the table.

"Hey!" Proclaimed a tiny voice.

"Sorry, didn't see you there," Charles apologized to the spider sitting on his nice kitchen chair.

He saw his newspaper open and folded right to the crossword, the best part. He picked it up and there was a tiny arachnid crawling back and forth across the horoscopes. Charles presumed it was examining its future. Sadly the crossword was already fully completed with an awkward white-yellow looking fluid. At the very least it was precise hand, or more appropriately, leg-writing. Charles set the paper back and decided to listen to the conversations on the table among the close-knit spider groups. They talked about watching a horror movie later that night, titled, "Beware Itsy Bitsy," that they had read in the TV guide. It was rerunning. Of course, because that was Badwick's luck. They talked about how the film was going to hit home and be emotionally involving. Then they talked a lot about the philosophical concepts involved, but Charles couldn't follow. Instead he tried to make conversation elsewhere, to fit in with his new roommates.

"So, noticed the egg sacks in the mug over there. You guys ever get together just to have a massive spider orgy?" Charles said almost jokingly.

"Oi! Who do you think we be? Regular slacking, don't-care-who-sees-us hippie-folk? Not us, we may have a 'laxin' morning, but we get to the grindstone soons enough!" BR1 said in his usual insulted tone.

"Sorry BR1, didn't even see you there," Charles continued to make amends.

"Didn't see? Oi! There goes again saying we all looks the same!" BR1 scoffed.

Charles let out a loud, grated sigh of nervous nature. There was an awkward day ahead of him.

Where Doth the Bark Grow?

I'm sitting in a shop, my eyes barely open, but I think I can make out her face. She's so excited to see me. It's kind of funny, because I'm just a regular guy, nothing too special. My hair is straight and clean, but my coat is a little plain. But after we speak for a while, show what I can do, I hop in her car. It's a rush; I have never driven in such a nice car. I've been in them before of course, but usually it is a dark and tough ride. Plush seats are new to me, but I like them, and I really like the wind in my face, but it makes me feel all off-balance.

I walk in her home. It's none too big, and she seems to share various rooms that are all over this place. A hall of doors makes me a little scared, but I learn which one is hers. And when she places her hand on my head I get so comfy and warm. I had brothers and sisters that did this, but this experience was a little different My siblings left me long ago, going on with their own lives.

Things seem so wonderful right now and when she watches her box with the moving people I wonder how it works, but mostly I just lay on the couch with my head on her lap. I love this lady.

Things don't stay that way for too long though. There are little things this girl does I pass off, but they are strange, scary things. One time she yelled at me for going to the bathroom in her home. I guess I have no place doing that. But why? Isn't it my home too? Our home? It doesn't matter though. I just tell her I'm going outside to find a bathroom, which makes her angry when she's watching her box. I whimper a little and lower my head, because she never yells at me, but she just tells me she is stressed out, and I understand.

I hate to interrupt her box-watching, but I can't tell what she sees in there, with her glazy eyes. It must be important, because she pushes me away a lot when I want to play a little catch with her. So I sit, alone. Oh, oh, but sometimes a bug crawls in the house and I kill it for her. She thinks its gross, but its kind of fun. I love this lady.

Now I'm feeling bigger, more confident, I'm living my own life. But she must sense it because she yelled at me the other day for sampling the couch. Sandalwood, oddly enough. Not really that tasty, but oddly pleasant to chew. Kind of like her rubbery flip-flops, but she hit me when I did that. I used to play around like that all the time, she never hit me then. My bottom hurt the whole rest of the day, and even though I tried to stop the tears, I couldn't. I just kept whimpering. I didn't understand, did she not love me like I did her? Maybe she is still stressed out.

Now she's putting something on my head, and it's tight, like I can't breathe. She says it's to make sure I'm safe, but I don't feel very safe with it on. Like I'm being watched all the time, 'cause now everyone knows my name. "Everyone" meaning my friends at the park. They are just like me, but I don't get to hang out long, because she drags me away after no time at all.

Sometimes when I'm sleepy she still make me walk, and my throat feels so tight my eyes start to escape my little face, so I have to keep walking 'til my legs start to burn and give out on me. My tongue hangs from my mouth, because I'm so exhausted, but she thinks I'm happy. I am though, even when I can never be alone and do my own stuff, and even when she pulls me along. Sometimes it hurts, but I still love this lady.

She keeps teasing me now. It's sort of funny, but a little queer too. She holds my favorite treats above my head, and right when I reach out to grab, she pulls them away. Then she uses her mean voice on me, controlling and harsh. I just want my yummy treats, but they keep going, up and down. Eventually she gives up and walks away, saying I'm dumb. She puts the treats in a box in a high away place. I haven't found anything high enough to stand on yet.

Now I'm not bad anymore. I listen to everything she says, even when I don't want to, just like when we walk together. I don't try to go outside on my own anymore, this place is fine enough. I quit my hobbies for her, she likes that. It makes everything easier. Besides, she keeps this dry crunchy stuff in a bowl for me, probably cereal, something healthy. Not very chewy like a sandalwood-flavored couch, but pretty good anyway.

Now I sit when she says, I lay when she says; I even greet her with a shake when she already knows me. And I get to sleep in her bed. It's a lot softer than my small blanket. Then that warm hand lands on my head and rubs, boy it feels good. I love my master.

Things are well. My master seems happier, yet distant. She'll rub my head when I lay on her, and I'll grab things for her that she accidentally throws over and over. She must have a funny twitch. She doesn't really seem like she watches her box that much anymore. It's on, and there she is on the couch, but she's not really even looking at it.

Now there is this strange man with ugly smells here. He's been here before, and whenever I try to talk to him, to say *hello*, my master tells me to shut up. Finally I do, but I don't think his smell is any better. I don't like this man. He's big, real big, bigger than my master even. And whenever he is around my master seems different.

The other day my master and the man with ugly smells were sitting on the couch pressing their faces together. At first I thought they were fighting, but I remember my master doing that to me. It wasn't nearly as aggressive, but it felt nice. I thought I would play too, but they pushed me away. My back hit the corner of the table, and it hurt in my bottom more than anything.

I scampered off, leaving my toys by the couch where I dropped them. Even my bone shaped toy. Doesn't taste like a bone, but I love it a lot, just like I still love my master.

I don't get to sleep with my master anymore, she found someone else warm to keep her company. There's not much room up there, so I look for my old bed. There's a big fallen jacket on my blanket, and a shoe. I don't know where the other one is, so I just pull the big thing off my blanket. It takes a while, but my old blanket makes it worth it. It's itchy and rough, but comfy, like always. It's awfully chilly tonight.

I don't really see the man with ugly smells anymore. I like that. But my master isn't around much either these days. I don't like that. She comes home tonight late and heads right to bed. She doesn't even bother to turn her head at me, but that's okay, she's busy, and I love my master. I paw at her door, but there is no answer. Another night on the blanket might be good for me. Maybe I'm bad again.

I'm sitting at my bowl looking for my tasty, crunchy cereal. It isn't there. There are tiny pieces, kind of like specks of dust, but empty otherwise. It's strange. There is usually food there. Course, I have not seen my master since yesterday. Maybe she'll come home tonight. I'd like to see her. Maybe we could play catch.

I'm looking at my bowl again, but no matter how hard I concentrate, it doesn't fill up, and I can't reach the tall wooden boxes on the wall. I look at the door from my bowl, excited and waiting, but the door stares back at me, menacing. Looks like the sun is going bye-bye, and the shadows on the short hall to the door make me nervous. A small whimper slips out of me, even though I try to be strong and stop it. Master isn't coming home tonight. My tummy hurts.

I jump up from my little bed and wiggle my bottom. I hear clicking! The kind of clicking you hear inside those moveable wooden walls, um doors. I'm standing, my mouth salivating and my tongue lashing out intently. Oh boy, oh boy, here she comes, and we'll play fetch, and we'll watch the fuzzy box, and we'll eat. Oh, I hope she brought leftovers, like that bag of beef jerky she brought home once. The clicking sound fades, and I tilt my head, cheated. No open door? I lower my head and sulk back to bed. It must have been the people next door, but they are not my master. It is getting harder to love my master.

She finally comes home, but we don't talk about our days, because she just collects a bunch of stuff and heads for the door. I have to chase after her yelling to get her attention. She looks like she feels horrible, and we hug. It's the warmest hug ever. I eat heartily and slobber all over the place. We even go for a walk! Things are going to change this time around, I know it. The man with ugly smells will stay gone, and it will be me and my master again.

We don't walk far though. Twice around the block, but that is enough. I missed the feeling in my legs and the breeze in my hair. We walk upstairs to the same old home and I rush to my fake bone with dreamy eyes. She tells me she is busy, but will be back. I know she will be. I wash my hair while I wait for her to return from her room with the big comfy bed.

She is angry, terribly angry with those fierce eyes. She looks so much like a hungry dragon with those eyes. I cower, but I don't know why. She yells and yells at me. I yelp as she grabs my neck-band stiffly and pulls. The feeling of suffocation returns. And my neck-band itches so much I can hardly stand it. And oddly, my worries change to wondering when my last bath was. Not that being dirty isn't fun. Or so I think, before she shoves my face fully into something. My nose is overpowered by the scent and my eyes water. It is a strong, stinky smell. I try to pull away, but my face just gets pushed in deeper, but at least I can't breathe anymore. Soon I get released, and the pulsations in my small head disappear, but the odor doesn't. It's on my face somewhere, but I can't scratch it away no matter how hard I rub.

She tells me I deserve it for being bad. I couldn't help it, there was nowhere else for me to go. She is never here to allow me outside anymore. She slams the door behind her and I'm trapped. I can't open the door; the metal piece is too slippery and

hard to grip, so my home keeps shrinking. At least the bed is
here, but I don't sleep there. I'm afraid she'll find my hair in the
fabric and hit me again, or worse. So I lie next to the door and
wait. If only she would come back, I'd do anything for her. I'd
bring back anything she threw, even if it hurt to carry, even if it's
too heavy for me to lift. I want to make you happy my master.
Why don't you love me?

It is many hours later, and the smell grows hard to my
face. It lives there now, and eats my dreams. It's the last place I
can run, but now even that abandons me. I stare, looking at
nothing really. I am mostly trying to not think about that intense
itching around my neck band. It tingles, tries to hijack my body,
but I resist. Master used to tell me scratching there was bad.
Soon my muscles tense, and I almost sweat. It feels like tiny
bugs crawling all over my head, trying to take control, to destroy
my mind once they drill inside.

Finally I take it no more. I scratch, feeling very good.
Soon it starts to hurt, and my hair is pulling out, but I keep at it.
Soon my neck-band starts to loosen and fray, but I keep on
scratching until I feel moisture. I don't want to stain my master's
floor. I feel confident I tracked the bugs down and killed them.
They didn't have any place wandering my head, and without their
own home they were no good. My loose neck-band lets me
breathe like I haven't for a long time. I can't believe I didn't
notice how stale the air around here was before.

I leap back and stealthily scurry out when the door flies
open. I guess my master doesn't notice me. She's with the man
with ugly smells again, and she is stumbling all over hiccuping.
He's touching her everywhere and I feel like I should attack, to
protect my master. My hair stands on end and my teeth show,
but then a fresh air takes over the stale one, and my wound
reminds me of my loose neck-band. Maybe I've been wrong all
along. Maybe my master's real form has been invisible to me,
and all it took was a tiny bit more air to clear my head.

It stings a little, but now I know my master was wrong.
I'm good, and I always have been. I turn and see the source of

this pained realization. The big wooden panel. The door. It looks closed, but it's not. There is a crack of light piercing the darkness, and the seal is broken. I walk, smelling carefully and push against the door. It budges. I do it again, and finally I can pass through. I sit for a little bit, wondering if it is alright to leave alone, but I snap out of it when I hear a repetitious pounding from inside home. Maybe the man with ugly smells is showing her how it feels to be treated the way I was. My decision is made, and I tug at my neck-band until it snaps. The release is so great, I feel as though I can jump so much higher, run so much faster, and finally relax. Because I am who I am, and my master... She... Didn't fit with me.

I've seen the ins and outs of moving around this large place outside home on our walks, so I manage my way outside. I wander away from the place darker than night sky. But the moon looks down at me sadly. Do not cry moon, I am okay.

I travel for a long time, but I'm sure it isn't too far for her to find me, so I keep moving. Only when my feet feel numb, rough, and full of blisters do I stop. I see a short wooden bed by me, but instead I decide to sleep by the nearby tree. The wind billows and bites me. It covers me like an itchy blanket, but I don't even feel it through my worrisome satisfaction. My eyes feel heavy now and I sleep. I don't know what to love anymore.

I wake up in a new blanket. This time it's leaves. I look around, but my caregiver is gone. Thank you moon. I look up, and a tree has bared itself down upon me. It must have battled away the wind, sacrificing itself, just for me. And now I sleep on its battle scars of various reds, oranges, and browns. Or so I think. I can't really see them in distinct color, but I remember my old master telling what various shades of gray looked like. I'm hungry now.

I've been here for several visits with Mr. Moon. I talk to him sometimes, but he doesn't say much. He's always sad about something. Mr. Sun is a lot more cheery, and he is friends with many more people. These people stand around this place, and sit on the wooden bed, but I don't pay them much attention. I have bad memories. But I also grow tired of searching for little bugs to kill and munch, and chewy gross-tasting papers by a big metal can. So I decide I will talk with them, and maybe I'll get better food.

I interrupt one man's game of catch with his friend. His friend is angry at this, but the man tells him to calm down. I look up with my best happy face, but he gets frightened and backs away, leaving his tossing toy. I sit confusingly and get that itch again. It has been coming back. I pull my arm back and stare at the end. It's gooey gross-smelling pus stuff again. Bits of my skin too. I hope my neck is okay, but I get a mind-ache more and more these days.

I muster up my courage and find other people who look happy like my face, but everyone gets really nervous and avoids me. I don't know why. People are staring, or trying not to stare, maybe. Finally someone approaches me, and he is wearing this beautifully spotless white suit. I approach him gently and sniff. He smells nice, familiar. He sort of smells like me.

He carefully picks me up and I try to lick his face, but he holds me so far away. Still, I trust this man. I pant excitedly and my mouth starts to foam a little from the entire new experience paring with the hunger and future food. He places me in the back of a big car, just as white as he is, and he seals it up.

I look around and see other people holing themselves in the back of the car too. This reminds me so much of my youth. Somehow, I find myself missing my mommy. Things were so easier back then, and the cars seemed so much less dark in her arms. Now I might be the last of my family. But at least I'm with people just like me, and we're together, through thick and thin.

The rough ride ends and we clammer about. Some are shaking and trying to shove themselves through the back wall of the car. Others start to bare their teeth as the sole line of defense. Others were simply in a state of wonder like me. I can tell a lot about my comrades already.

The door opens, and even the toothy ones have a hard time not flinching against the light. There stand many other Men in White Suits. Their hats shade their heads, making them faceless. We are led out. Some are pulled in with long rods that hook themselves to my angrier acquaintances. Others try to make a run for it, but they only end up with a fence closing in around them. They too get a reprimand from the rod. The rest of us see this, and we feel their shady eyes staring us down, so we pacify ourselves to their whims.

We walk into the ominous building. They document us all and we are led to many different sections of the building. I never see some of my comrades again, but most make it to where I am. The Men in White Suits close a metal grate behind me and I find my new home.

Things aren't that bad now. Actually, It's about the same as before, only without the mean lady. It's good she does not come for me. Never can live on my own wherever I want I suppose. Not my kind. But I get my own bowl for water and crunchy cereal bits. They are a bit drier than I'm used to, but it's always plentiful. My home is much smaller, and it's sort of like the building I lived before, only with other people like me on all sides. No wooden walls either. It's also a lot cleaner, and I'm teaching myself how to read the stuff they paste my floor with. There are these pictures with this cat, I don't know what it's saying, because I don't understand cat, but it looks funny.

When I came in here originally, they cleaned up my neck with cool bandaging. It stings at first and they hold me down, but after it is all over, I feel great. The itching is gone, and I have funny wrappings around my head. They keep saying something about the cone, but I don't know what they mean.

I can't go outside whenever I want, but I get to anyway almost every day. And I have a lot of new friends all around me. We talk a lot at night after the Men in White Suits leave.

There is even one man in a white suit who is my friend. We're not much alike, but we sure have fun together. I never see his face, but he talks to me soothingly and places his warm hand on my head. I shut my eyes when he does that and I feel what it's like not to be lonely anymore. We even play tug-of-war and catch when I go outside. I love my new master.

Shortly after I arrive I huddle back in my metal-mesh home. There are strange people here. They are shorter than the Men in White Suits and they wear sticky, brightly colored clothing. They are squealing and running around making loud noises. They smell dirty compared to my new master. I back further into my metal mesh home and stare with wide-eyes. My breathing speeds up and my bottom stops its tiny shake.

They run around poking their sticky, dirty fingers in the holes of our homes, and others rattle their foundations. Many of my friends are happy to see this change in characters, licking the sugary substances off fingers and yipping. I don't feel like them. I get sick in my stomach and shut my wide eyes tight. I hope they don't see me and drag me off from my very own home like she did, so they can toss me away and forget. Everything starts to shake. The noises are louder, almost deafening, and I grit my teeth. I try my hardest not to show them, but lips peel open and a dangerous grin shoots out. No! Darkness and earthquakes. Tense muscles. I'm good. I'm very good.

It's exhausting. My double life wears thin. I'm so giddy and energetic, until the gates release and the little ones run in. Then my mind roars and I act poorly, almost mean, maybe… Bad. I breathe heavily after its over, and I begin to recall. My friends get taken from their homes and they look like they are expecting a bright future. They lick vigorously at the little ones' faces. And I never see them again.

Those ones know not what they mean. Calling our tiny homes, "cages." I don't know if it's true or not, but I think maybe it's a fort keeping bad people out. They can't touch me in here. And a little acting keeps the clean Men in White Suits from releasing me to the little ones' touch. I don't know which way or how those taken go, but they leave me. It's okay, because soon their homes get new owners, and I meet all sorts of interesting people just like me. It is a safe place, and I love my new master.

My new master is in disappointment and is so for a while. I think this anyway, because he doesn't talk to me much anymore. Not since several new tenants move in however far back. I miss the fun we have together and that warm, warm hand on my head. Those new tenants are a bit younger than me, more energetic, so I guess it makes sense. Who has time to play at this age? Helps me a little too, because most strangers pass by me nowadays. I'm left alone to talk with people around me and the Men in White Suits, which I like. Besides, it's harder for me to walk around anyway, my body aches in a lot of places.

I think I'm safe from the strange people, but today a new man walks in, his face is all wrinkly, just like a couple of the guys who live here. He looks like he has trouble walking too. He looks house to house, until he stops by mine. He leans over and peers in. He has this hoarse voice. He's calling me *little guy*, even though I have a name. I get many different names from people, but I'm pretty sure I have a real one. I can't remember what it is though. The Men in White Suits are taking me to this man with dry riverbeds in his face. He's holding me and I don't like it. This wrinkly man smiles and rubs his face against my side. It feels weird, almost soothing, but still I am wary.

He hobbles toward the big door I always see other strangers exit. The door my people go through but never back. I don't want to leave, I don't want to. What if this wrinkly man is tricking the Men in White Suits? Why doesn't my new master stop him? I panic, and twist my head. My dull nails push, but I'm held tight. I do the only thing worthy.

I bite him.

My teeth sink into his likewise dry hands, but the flesh is thin and loose. Warm iron-tasting water slowly draws into my jowls. The taste is bitter, but well worth it. I freefall and land with a lump. It hurts my bottom, but I manage to get up and limp toward home. I almost get there when I trip on my side. I was knocked to the ground. Blows come my way that are more shocking than painful. A man in a white suit pummels me and says I'm bad, really bad. I whimper and try to roll away, but he holds me tight on my back. I feel like hyperventilating.

When I finally get home, I feel horrible. I didn't mean to be bad, but I like it here, safe in my metal-mesh box. The other people here turn away from me, but I know what they think. They don't understand. I see the wrinkly man cussing and holding his hand in wrappings. The wrappings were white I thought, like the men's suits, but it is a strange shade. Red if I remember. The Men in White Suits are consoling him with hands on shoulders. It works well.

Soon the wrinkly man leaves, but first he shoots me a dirty, foul glance. I feel safe again. But now the Men in White Suits are in front of my metal mesh home with heightened whispers. I don't know the meanings of what they say, but they look down on me like I'm bad. A fight looks to break with their hands waving like that. Finally they slow themselves and my new master lowers his head, expressionless, and stares at me out of the corner of his eye. I'm glad he is still communicating with me. He hasn't forgotten after all. He nods slowly and the Men in White Suits walk away, as well as my new master.

At nightfall the people here yammer. Some speak of freedom, others gossip, but mostly they talk about my actions today. I pay them no heed, but some of the folks who have lived here for some time say I shouldn't have done what I did. I ask them why, but they've no explanation for me. All they know is for some reason, most people leave through the door toward the full metal-mesh homes of new tenants. Bad people tend to leave through a door opposite, toward sparser metal-mesh homes. Neither door seems to ever lead back here. I decide to make an early night after all the excitement. Seems I sleep more and more these days.

The next day I see the Men in White Suits pass along the metal-mesh homes, and with them as always, my new master. Sadly though, he doesn't look at me. I'm looking forward to coming outside today, like I don't do much, but nobody comes to help unlock my door. It sticks often. I sit around waiting more and more, panting in anticipation, but the day goes by uneventful. No strangers even visit today. I think maybe I'll eat and stretch for a while.

Nightfall comes again; I can sense the strange look of outside this time. It has been a while, but I can still remember that at least. I don't see the Men in White Suits leave, but I do see someone else come in. He's not wearing black, but maybe brown or beige? I don't see his face too well, much like the Men in White Suits, but he smells of something funny familiar. Sort of like the people here, but singed maybe?

He's approaching my metal-mesh home, helping me open it. I'm a little afraid, like I always am. I would have to work on my courage again one day. Despite that, I've been itching to play outside all day, and I happily saunter out with my tongue wagging. I start scampering toward the door outside when I feel my air missing. I feel a pull and almost bite my tongue. I look around, somewhat frantic, and see a pole near my neck. The pole is being held by this Man in Beige who surpasses my strength. I give up fighting, walking side-by-side instead. I see the door near sparse spots growing larger, shadows covering my small frame. The door is dusty, and it squeaks when the Man in Beige shoulders it open.

The room is messy, with all sorts of tools I've seen used before; brooms, empty boxes, pails, and this big strange machine in the middle of the room. It must be a machine anyway, because it looks like it has a lot of metal parts, big and small all holding each other in place. This is one object that is unfamiliar to me. The Man in Beige holds tightly to the pole, struggling with a lever that pops a door open in the middle of the big device. How silly, the door was absent to me earlier. The Man in Beige picks me up, loosens the ties on my neck and tosses me in.

The door quickly shuts me in, the whispers of my friends in the other room fade away. There is a window in the door, but it is small and foggy. I step around and don't feel right. There is a strong odor here that's even more funny familiar. Like singe smells lying with a hint of the people outside. I don't like it here.

It's toasty warm, yet solid and tough. Gone are my funny floor-coverings of talking cats. And I had only recently taught myself what they meant too.

This must be my punishment for being bad, isolation. I'm learning my lesson, I'll be good now. I said that before, but really I mean it this time, please. I'll live with the wrinkly man if that will make me good again. Let me see people and sit somewhere soft. No more tiny box.

Suddenly my twisting and turning in the box halts when I hear a big churning sound. Clank clank. The man with beige is still be out there and he's letting me go after finding my lesson. I wag my tail softly, trying to compose myself, when a spray of smoke strikes my face.

I back away and squint my eyes. Smoke is filling the box. It's on fire! I run to the door and claw at the tight seal. There is nowhere to grip, so I pound and yell for help. Can the Man in Beige not hear me? I'm screaming so loud. The door is still stuck. Help! I've got to get out of this, away from the fire. I try grabbing the sides, but no luck befalls me. I try ramming it, but I can't get enough push. Beginning to feel exhausted.

My muscles don't hurt anymore, but I feel like I'm suffocating. In a good way, if that makes any sense. I'm starting to feel sleepy now, and suddenly this place doesn't seem so bad. Everything is cloudy and comfy. In fact, it feels like the most comfortable place in the world.

I stagger back to the center of the room, almost blind from the smoke, and circle around a couple of times. I lay arm over arm and gently place my head atop them. I breathe in deep as I can, and momentarily think back on my life. I did some bad things, but I feel like I did a lot of good too. And then I start thinking about my mommy. I miss her, but maybe we'll see each other again someday.

My eyes are so heavy. I'm going to sleep now. I think when I wake up tomorrow morning I'll convince my new master to play catch with me, using that ball with the eight plastic pieces. That'll be fun. I love my new master.

How Serene the Sky

We are a strong force dedicated to the whim of our lord. He is well-known and kind. With his dynasty all began, and with its end, so too shall we all. What greater a ruler than he? With his watch, he lends his green thumb to crops and they grow infinitely larger. He brings us vision clear and into hearts of criminals fear. Even in sleep his nobility shines through in the glowing cheeks of the content wife. Many a man goes mad at merely seeing the full of her face, uncovered by the darkness of shadow. Their greedy desires for our lord's main host finding truth through a glance.

It is then that we laugh at such mortals while tipping our cups to drink, that we stumble and fall to slumber, our bodies laid out widely on our post, from the exhaustion of mind and our steadfast guard.

We do not always protect our noble lord; for he built his castle so high aloft, nay, beyond the sky that his wards may not so much as touch him, much less those of less valid occupation. At times, despite our tone, precise skill, despite our loyalty, he requests our leave for an unobstructed view of his peoples and lands below. It is then that he beams proudest, knowing of his great kingdom.

I am a noble ronin who has been under servitude for decades. For such dedication, my gracious lord has given me the long sought title of Nimbus, the anvil of the gracious sky. It is so for I am soft and gentle, while also being responsible enough to bring down the hammer. My real name matters not now. I attend my lord's every beck and call, but mostly I keep command of my young samurai charges, keeping them in tip-top shape. There is no denial, however, that I occasionally abuse those powers given unto me.

On more than one occasion have I terrified the peasants below with my harsh taxes. I know not what causes these outbursts, perhaps it is merely the outlook of man, under a lord, with a right to enforce and perhaps test it. At times I show them the danger without their lord's touch, a punishment for their inappreciative ways. It is when his green thumb leaves and their crops fall they bow to him again and know truly his generous strength.

Of course, my lord can be too gracious with his presence. In some parts of his land he refuses to leave for days, to take in all wonder of men, women, and children working subtly for his causes. In other places he visits, for my master travels often, he will sit for long periods of time, escaping our protection, and sits tanning himself gently. He enjoys descent from his palace to sit on steps shortly down. His near heart is so warm that the heat grows too intense. The curses of jealous peasants away from his smiling eyes and the extended stay elsewhere cracks the land and burns the villagers of any well meaning and soon complain of him. The omens overtake their clear thought, and our lord, noble and kind, will shrug to take his leave, and let his wife take watch with her full-bodied, tender eyes.

Naturally, a mortal is a mortal, and so our cosmic-bound lord is subject to heated emotions like ourselves. Sometimes when peasants ignore his strengths or complain that his rule is poor, his anger will burn even our backs, armor-clad as they are. He will send us to deal forth harsh punishment, no matter how trite the ordeal.

Usually we spar each other, toppling the loser and pulling our swords to their neck to claim defeat. Then all would be forgiven, and we would down another bottle each for a grand night of challenges. But it is when I feel I have to dole out our stored need for battle upon the peasants that I sometimes question my servitude, despite my overflowing passion.

We line up in great numbers and pull our swords from sheathes. We bring them up, their silver glinting, and bring them down many a time. Mostly we simply scare the people lower in the ranks of lordship, bringing our swords down upon the land, the speed of our refined skill so great the friction burns a hole in the ground. And it is our policy to never hit the same spot twice, for we know our swords have so much to taste. Sometimes we strike trees and tall buildings, for their foolish attempts to climb to our lord. And when we occasionally fell a peasant, he shakes and rattles under the impact and babbles nothingness, much like the tower of a similar fame. Our aura's pierce the untrained body and leave terrible knowing scars as a message to all.

They put that unfortunate individual on their television talk shows, and their magazines, and our lord beams brighter than ever. Understandably, there are networks which solely dedicate themselves to our actions, and many hours elsewhere are lent to describing our lord's current activities. A sort of religious spectacle, but our lord is not quite a god, though I say so in hushed whispers. The peasants even have a code sentence, which all peasants under his rule know. It serves as an introduction, a sort of miniscule brotherhood to break to the ice.

Humorously, we often get the blame for bad things, for our lord is clever and covert in such ways. And I am happy to do it, for he gives me a great palace in the sky to rest my head, and my own troupe of soldiers who answer to me. Once, but once, did our lord give me the hand of his wife in dance while he slept. It was the most gorgeous night, and every detail I recall in my fluttering heart. I swore my battle hand would fall frail from her calm. Even the tides sought to touch her, but they are too pitiful even now to do it.

Often we will train in public view, our blows trading at such speeds as to create furious light shows. There have been tributes to us in cheap imitation, works of fire, shot skyward toward our castles, but they fall pathetically short, and no more glorious is their blast than our own. It is when their works of fire are useless that we amuse the peasants most. Donned in armor of high durability and light weight, we are able to change shape, through our studies of anatomy. It takes incredible discipline, but we may take the shape of rabbits or dragons or cars or nuclear mushrooms or birds or peasant faces or ice cream sundaes or even nothing in particular as we please. The last one is my newest recruit's specialty. He claims he is creating art, but it lacks practicality, so he is the subject of many nights drunken laughter.

Those below in rank wish to touch us, and sit in our palaces of the sky, to shift their steady shapes, but it is futile. Their will is weak. They have built devices which try to place their feeble hands on our soldiers. Us, the warriors of his lordship. It is often in their grandiose attempts that they awaken us with pounding headaches, and our roars rot their guts to queasiness. They promptly run off leaving us with chuckling sighs.

Despite the pleasure of serving one without measure, eventually my arms grow weary and my mind tires of drink, and I wish to relax. On these rare occasions I seek out an empty field, traveling for hours in which to lay. This particular one is tricky, for plains open nicely onto a rickety bridge. I attempt not to fall, and remain high and noble, steadfast and adamant to find my favorite spot on the field to simply breathe. When I make it to the hill that towers slightly over the long-grass plains I find that someone has already beaten me there, but no matter, for I rest along with them. They find my presence unsatisfactory, for my sheer renown is enough to shadow over the hillside, but still I sit in attempted ignorance.

I imagine the feel of wheat grinding in my teeth, and regret not picking any for my venture, but I'm too lazy now to tread back down the pasture. So I sit near a tree and watch the serene beauty of these lands. I am always so preoccupied with those free to the skies and the pale blue that rests up there with peasant dreams. Sometimes it is nice to relax and meditate on the nature of earthbound things. The simplicity of a toad near a creek and the standing grass that looks to the trees for guidance.

The man beside is begging me to shift my shape. I shrug off his requests. I close my eyes lightly and breathe in deep, when I feel it. A stronger rush of air into my lungs than usual. It is faint, but my senses are sharply in tune with all. It grows now, and my eyes open to anticipate his coming. Each blade of grass below the hillside, short and tall, waves and bows to his presence, those who do not are pushed aside. He is hiding well within those pastures, slinking around like the tiger, but not even the greatest spy can leave every blade of grass unturned. I see him now, faintly, for he fades with his surroundings. His battle aura betrays him, making his location known. More important than that, however, is his legend, for he is wind.

I stand to prepare myself, as I place my hand upon my silver glinting sword. My thumb readies itself to thrust my sword from its holdings. Rigid as a statue, I feel his energy flowing all around me, but the peasant near me is too foolish to give care. He lies on his back and smiles; I leave no wonder in my mind as to why they constantly die.

Wind is a wretch of a foe, when he isn't whistling, he is roaring, which makes his approach all the more fearsome due to his tendencies. When my men hear that distinct whistle, we all pause in our actions and wait to see if we are dreaming in day, for after the whistle there lies the fallen. He is nothing more than a disloyal renegade, whom constantly disregards our lord's generosities. Wind washes away the gentle warmth of our lord's heart, and strikes hardest in those places where our lord is lacking. Our lord is mortal, he can only do so much, he can only be so many places, and his warriors are of only so many numbers, we have tried our damnedest to stop Wind's belligerent ways.

I tug on my sword and am almost put off balance by the approach of Wind's cold heart. As I see him practically glide uphill with his calm demeanor, I remind myself that his appearance is tricky. He too alters his shape, but while we work on our forms for peace, he works his for destruction. Tornadoes, hurricanes, and typhoons are all simple tasks for him, and I have seen laid to rest many of my comrades under his speedy, raw hatred. One on one would be difficult, but I was my lord's Nimbus, the anvil by Wind unmovable.

He stops now before me and rolls his head back and forth. He looks down on me with much disrespect and slowly pulls out his blade as well. It is dull and shoddy in appearance, but much like him, in truth it would never be sharper, with gems ornate and glowing dimly from the hilt. He spins it round several times, likewise slow and intimidating. His face grows fierce and my blade runs true, stopping his advance. A whoosh of battle energy washes away the warm heart's feel once more, and I am chilly within.

We trade blows left to right, and his legend grows might prevalent in my mind. Our lord had told us tales of Wind, which for our pillage of the land to strike down the tall trees threatening our lord, nature has intervened and created an unstoppable samurai to deftly deflect our complete control. He is not so much immortal as he is regenerative. Our lord himself has slain him many a time, but he always ends up coming back somewhere. Wind always seems to have an upper hand. He can pass by us without notice, he cannot be held for he slips through any bindings, and when he decides to confront us he tends to decimate us utterly, giving no care to the peasants he harms in the process.

Yes, created from toppled trees, humorous it is then that those same tall trees are the only things that seem to slow the nefarious Wind. It is as though he was made solely to mock us more than harm us. Stop the empire, and Wind slows to a grinding halt. Expand the empire, and Wind grows strong enough to shrink it.

Our blades slip back into sheaths. We stand for a moment, in a haze, my bodily fluids misty as they flow out. I do not yet feel the grasp of death, but he has dealt the winning blow.

With a smirk I am sent reeling back, and my body loses form from its samurai shapes.

I float back toward my palace in the sky and I know that even though I am Nimbus, anvil of the sky, head samurai to my lord who reigns over all, Clouds cannot win out against Wind.

Meanwhile, a small child tells his mother I'm made of cotton candy.

The Bee that Loved Music

Once again the deafening buzz was audible throughout the hive, Beesdale regretted to notice as he dropped off another batch of newly collected nectar. As Beesdale scuttled ever more deeply into the catacombs, he grew ever more displeased. Beesdale hated his hive. It had interesting décor to be sure, but the encasement of dim-lighting and unrythmic, nigh-indecipherable hums and buzzes that echoed off the tightly enclosed walls negated any quality elements it held. Beesdale longed for a grand utopia. A place of relative quiet, away from the hive, peaceful and separate from the hustle and bustle of the Pollen-Collector's life. But for now, Beesdale had to put up with what he had, a life full of day-in day-out humdrum. It truly dulled his senses, which is why he proceeded to accidentally bump into one of his female coworkers from the honey-producing division.

"Oh, terribly sorry," apologized Beesdale.

"No worries, I barely saw you there," Replied back the Honey Producer. "I see you're here to drop off a nectar shipment. How are things?"

"Terrible. It's always the buzz, buzz, buzz that screams inside my mind. Makes it hard to concentrate."

"Oh I don't know, all the chattering is kind of fun, especially the gossip. Plus, it makes the day mill on by. Besides…" She continued on about something, but Beesdale just sat there in a trance-like stare. He may have been mostly honest, but he wasn't a complete cad. So Beesdale stood there praying for it all to end, when fate answered his call.

"Alroight, whut's goin' on 'ere?! Whut're you lot doin' then eh?" A large warrior bee plopped beside Beesdale, the displeasing sensation of the burly warrior's black and dingy yellows rubbing against his snapped him to attention.

"What Beezy said," Followed a smaller, yet still intimidating fellow who landed near the more boisterous of the two.

"I was merely having a bit of conversation with the impeccable honey ladies. All business I assure you." Beesdale decided on the quickest lie he could, because he knew those two. Beezy and H-Comb, highly appointed warriors only in line authority-wise behind the queen and her always-by-side bodyguards. They had the sort of knack to always go looking for trouble, and find it.

"Oi, I thought I sawr you b'fore. You're one o'them worker bees. Didn't I tell ya he were one o'them worker bees H-Comb?" Beezy asked the small and ever-agreeable H-Comb.

"Yea, you tol' me palsy, I hoids it."

"You bes' get back workin', worker. Go on, I don' want to tell ya again. Get Collectin' already."

"I was just…" Beesdale valiantly failed an attempt at explanation.

"Whut's that? You not hears so well? You wants I should cut you some new ears?" H-Comb threatened.

"I'm going already," and with a stored sigh, Beesdale left the stressed situation back toward his designated job.

As Beesdale neared the exit of the hive, he thought to himself. He wasn't friends with that many who populated the hive. In fact, he barely even knew the names of most of the workers be bunked with. But that Beezy and H-Comb were easily antennae-bending in the worst way. He stopped short of the doorway outside, making a quick mental note to rank the power-drunk warriors' voices on the top of the worst noises list, right above drunken centipede jingles and scraping excess honey from defunct honeycombs.

Jumping from the hive his wings utilized and thrust him from "home." Short whiles later, Beesdale found bee gold, marigold that is. As he rested on flowers and took in their supple scent, he gazed briefly at the cleverly crafted circle that nature herself managed to supply in both regions practical and artistic. Work was to be done, however, and Beesdale continued on about his job, in the usual fashion, the rest of the day.

Once again Beesdale was jolted from slumber. As he stretched grumpily he looked around. The sleeping quarters for worker bees were impersonal and tightly-packed. From his dim vantage point he appeared to be the only one awake, everyone else sleeping in a mass of rumbles and snores.

"Third time tonight," whimpered Beesdale. "What's even the point of trying to sleep? Soon as one stops, louder snores start up."

And so Beesdale sat up and considered the option of becoming insomniac. He would finally read those exact pollen-producing guidelines, right in time for reviews. He had heard about someone who tried that, most of the workers say he went mad, others claimed he thought himself a bird and got eaten. Beesdale thought it all a rumor just dull enough to get him back to where he needed, with sleep in his eyes. As he fluffed out his short fur he prepared himself for a mighty powerful rest.

"Beesdale old pal!" Shouted a voice that startled Beesdale. "Can't believe you're up at this hour. I totally understand you buddy, who wouldn't look forward to another day in service to our royal queen? Wanna do some reps with me? Totally great for stretching out those pectorals and wing muscles."

"Heavens, not this," Beesdale moaned. It was Zwarm, always easy to pick out from a crowd. Considering their understanding of nature and advancements in socio-political studies, most of the workers bees thought they had a swell life. Zwarm was the epitome of this belief. Beesdale heard stories, against his will, from Zwarm, and they usually entailed incoming younger workers or his increase in pollen collection for the day. To be honest, if not for his steadfast dedications, Beesdale almost found his undying energy and loyalty contagious.

"Sorry, I don't follow."

"Listen, I'm sorry I snapped. I'm just so tired, I can't get a good night's sleep around here, and judging by the fact you're awake, I... Anyway, I was having such a nice dream. A place full of new sights and sounds, it was a paradise! But I kept waking up before the end."

"Oh man, I hear you, no good when that happens. Like those dreams you sometimes have about collecting pollen, and you never find out if you were top collector for the day? But hey, better to get up early than sleep late I always say! Gives you a lot more time to serve the glory of the hive. Today we'll be as busy as a... As a... Hmm... I forget the saying, but you know my point friend."

Such sentiments did little to raise Beesdale's spirits, or his attention span, as he was still quite tired. Beesdale almost had out a yawn and a further comment on his worries when Zwarm noticed the slight change in lighting about them.

"Oh no! Do you see that? When you notice the detail of the bunks, you know daybreak is coming." Zwarm said that last part off-hand, but Beesdale couldn't really see the difference. By the time Beesdale had gazed back down, Zwarm was already buzzing around rudely waking the other bees from sleep.

When Zwarm finally corralled the workers to the entrance of the hive, Beesdale had already stumbled his way groggily there. Numerous other workers joined him, as Zwarm quickly buzzed back to the bunks to make sure he had head count down. When Zwarm had finally settled, he was flustered all the more by the sight of the workers just standing around. As he squeezed his way past, he asked hurriedly why none of them were getting the move on.

That was, until he assumed the same slack-mandible expression the rest of the group acquired. They stood this way

for several moments, paralyzed with surprise. Around that time
Beezy and H-Comb scuttled up in a huff, after having heard that
honey-production was rapidly decreasing in chance of meeting
last month's total, in prime pollen season too.

"Eh, why isn' you workers working your work with
work!? 'Nuff lollygaggin'!" Shouted Beezy Authoritatively. He
had made extra sure to instill the forceful tone, but it went
unnoticed over the many unmoved workers.

H-Comb rushed amid the various workers trying to get
them to listen to Beezy. This worked to some extent, but ended
up finding the problem by seeing things himself. With admirable
haste H-Comb, despite his nature, gracefully flitted past everyone
to report back to Beezy.

"You wouldn'st believe it! Hoid little talkie-talks goin'
on with the woiker's, somethin' 'bout no chances. So I goes and
checks it out fer myself, see? I fly myself down there, not
believin' my eyes, but sure as our hive is great, and our stingers
sharp, the talkies are right!"

"Out with it already!"

"Flowahs Beezy, flowahs! They're all gone, like we'll be
if we don't do nothin'. Couldn't believe it! Pulled up I tells ya,
all of 'em! Looked like nice, fresh soil, coulda sworn I saw a
woim or sums about. But fresh soil, woims, or not; I never seen
any animal coulda done that. Sure, maybe a mole'll eat a flower,
but not a whole patch, no sir."

"Whut a predicament. Never 'eard o' any animal doin'
such lengthy work. Thems was lots o' flowers."

"Ya figures it was one of those, oh what are they...
Butterfly plots? Hoid they tried to pull somethin' couple months
back."

"Oi, hush yer theories, we need to think of a plan or the
Queen'll 'ave our 'eads, lest we starve first."

After hushed deliberation, they dusted off their
authoritative voices once more and instructed in a surprisingly
professional and order-inducing tone what would happen. Being
as there were no flowers around to get their jobs done, jobs which

made produce for the very fabric their society ran upon, they all had to work collectively and search far from their home, their hive. After setting up the rules, Beezy and H-Comb filled temporary roles as worker leads and had the bees set out with them.

"Boy, this sure isn't the... The uh... Oh, something's knees." Zwarm said in a lighthearted and likewise troubled tone as he started take-off.

"Centipede's knees?" Said another worker trying to fill in the blank.

"Ah, that must be it. This whole flower business isn't the centipede's knees today."

Beesdale was shocked for only a moment or two during the discovery. He was more in shock over the prospect of a potential day off. As usual, however, Beesdale's dreams went unrealized and would have to work even harder than usual under more supervision. And so Beesdale had flown closely behind his fellow workers.

The noise was ever more prevalent, buzzing drowning out any semblance of other sounds that usually graced nature. The group had passed by various trees and patches of grass never seen before. Despite the majestic nature of the tough, rippled bark on oaks, and the newly born sway of grass against the wind, Beesdale noted that everything looked the same, it just took longer to get to. About the time of that thought Zwarm had given the idea to start the group on reciting speeches the queen had given.

Zwarm was a mighty powerful speaker, but Beesdale couldn't handle it. He almost prayed a bird would pluck him from the sky, but he didn't really mean what he thought.

"In the name of neglectful nature, when will we find our nectar!?" Beesdale moaned out about halfway into the group's entrance into the queen's most recent motivational speech.

"Oi, you causin' trouble again eh little 'Dale?" Sneered Beezy.

"No respect, I'm tellin' ya Beezy. I sharpened the old stingah last night, let me teach him a lesson er two!" H-Comb excitedly waved his bottom in regards to his threat.

"Now, now, sirs. Let's not get ourselves a... Hmm... I'm really drawing a blank today. Anyway, don't get something in your bonnet is my point. We all need two things. Find those flowers so we can strengthen our powerful hive, a hive I remind you brothers, which has just finished a merger upon the death of Westwood Oaks Hive's queen. And we all need to do that by working together, while we bee ourselves." Zwarm paused after this motivated speech, before he started to chuckle. "Bee ourselves, ha ha, ooh..."

A series of groans removed the attention from Beesdale's complaints, and from his deception. For Beesdale could no longer handle the unintelligible ramblings of Beezy and H-Comb, the undying optimism and dedication of Zwarm, the gossip of the ladies at the honey-production area, and especially Aldrin. He wasn't quite sure why, he didn't even know if that was the worker's name, he had just seen him around once, and the way he chewed and twitched his head bugged him. Beesdale thought he spotted him in the crowd, and for no definable reason, Aldrin was the last straw in the entire fiasco, because this particular worker was chewing. Chewing on nothing, but he still acted like he had something in his maw. Beesdale did what he felt he had to do.

"Wasps! Look out! Wasps!"

Suddenly the cohesive band of brothers, that played off as though any would die for the other, scattered like a dropped sack of marbles. They flew every which way, and spotted nothing, but still some continued flight, such as Beesdale. He had zipped by in the same direction as several of his peers, but soon they slowed against Beesdale's quick pace. A pace not out of trained desire, but one of impulsive action. His tiny heart beat sharply against the walls of his chest as he passed by one tree, two trees, a couple of rocks, and on and on. When he felt like he was well beyond the group's authority, he paused for breath.

Surveying his surroundings, he noticed the trees all seemed alike. There were branches that twisted this way and that, but nothing too definable. Roughly the same amount of leaves, same color of bark, same rooted and unmoving lifestyles that made each spire create camaraderie with the other.

The Sun remained its usual sphere of flames untouchably skyward, peeking through the gaps in the leaves above. Those leaves held a dim silhouette of a lengthy caterpillar eating its way slowly through its standing.

Below held little interest with its brown-based coloring, with nothing but death as a blanket to those hidden within the scattered discards of the sturdy trees. It was those who took to the skies that survived, flitting among the suspended greenery and vast open spaces. Even the trees knew this to be true, always trying to reach higher and higher. But Beesdale had grown tired of his quick-reacted philosophy. His tiny heart slowed, as did his awareness. Before he decided to find the hive again or not, he would try to rest in this new place. Finding a gracious offering to rest, by way of a small part on the tree he stood, he laid himself to a deserved nap.

Beesdale found himself flying in darkness. His calls went unheard, echoing into a constant reverberation. This reverberation grew to a deafening level, and it almost shocked Beesdale from the pure dark skies. His flight preserved, however, and reverberations cleared through, as they yielded to a mysterious new sound.

Beams of light shot forth before he could react. He winced though remained unharmed, as the light passively passed through his being and back into darkness. These lights wavered and stretched into images. He couldn't see what was before him, but the flashing lights that dimmed the clarity of this vision seemed to be signaling upbeat ramblings ahead. Beesdale was a slave to the pulsations. He felt his body sway and move in such rhythms to be in tandem with the sounds and lights that brushed past.

About the time he felt he would truly touch this light, the static-like sound drowned out the visions. Darkness once more descended, and Beesdale couldn't keep up with the fading light. The hive was coming for him.

Beesdale witnessed himself in a small holding cell, until faded disorientation revealed it unlike a hive, but more treelike in nature. That was where he was, still in the tree he had chosen for slumber.

The echoes of his dreams remained in the background of regained comprehension. Investigating that matter, he slowly scuttled, as he peered over the edge of his individual fortress. Beesdale resisted the troubles of curiosity by succumbing to them.

Following the fragmented noise led to the source. Blended best he could with the bark, he was a fly on the wall, or rather a bee on the bark. It was a solemn creature, a lengthy body that owned even longer legs. It sat rubbing its tools, grating nastily against each other in a harsh fashion. He could tell the sound it produced was small and pack-like in creation. Besides, he could hear other such similar grated tunes.

Beesdale grew to appreciate this primitive culture, with their shelled wings, and their sense of an apparent social cohesion over distance, by way of scratched itching. They had the appearance of grasshoppers, and while he had never heard their tunes beyond the Sun's pass, he had heard rumors.

Under the continual chirping laid their true meaning. They knew how to relax, Beesdale admitted that, but their reason for gathering appeared to remain the same, night upon night. A group of gabby gals sitting on their leaves that shouted and complained of the heat. And if it wasn't the heat it was the bitter cold of a brisk fall. With such acknowledgements to their purposes, he found them nothing more than another group that didn't understand the concept of beauty. They were on a right path, but their group-think nature would keep them from greatness.

As he returned to his safe-hold, he renounced his hive and would seek out an existence alone. For a while anyway, to have clarity of thought. The night passed with grated tunes till moon's end.

Another night of poor sleep conflicted Beesdale's ability to strive for mental achievements. He started to slip back into the hive-like ways his brethren adhered to. Those leg whittlers didn't stop their discussions until well into the night, and the annoyances replaced fear with the sounds of birds, woodpeckers, soaring across Beesdale's holding. Even now the fear was subdued to the hunger within his belly. All he wanted was nectar, sweet, delicious nectar.

When he set out in the early morn, the forest had produced a cover in the form of thick fog. The moisture in the air weighted his wings, but he strived forward blindly. This same blindness afflicted every creature in the vicinity, however, and his weak, un-navigated path became his strength. Narrowly dodging trees, Beesdale's instincts led him to where the flowers may not have been, but should be.

A day out of practice led Beesdale to a vast desert laden with smoky fog. Beesdale normally would have tried to make light of an arid desert now sea-made by shifting weather, but instead thoughtlessly made a beeline toward a strange luminescent object in the distance.

He did find it a tad mysterious, the vast clearing almost limitless before him, but was perhaps more concerned with the oddly-shaped, thin, white trees that sparsely decorated the emptiness. Some looked fallen with vines growing down them, others forked off into a mere two symmetrical branches. Such peculiarity didn't slow the tug the glimmer had on his belly.

As he neared the enigmatic glimmer, he witnessed something beautiful. Beyond the forest and beyond the valley of fog that licked delicately at Beesdale's path, there was a dizzying array of variety in the form of plants. From what could be made out, very few looked similar to the other. Vines were mixed with small tree sprouts, were mixed with vegetables, were mixed with flowers! Beesdale raced toward the flowers, their purples, blues, and yellows taking hold of his colorless mind. He stretched his mandibles in anticipation.

With sudden force Beesdale slammed into nothingness. Confused, he tried again, and once more. Despite efforts, he remained ever-so-close, yet outside his reach. Exhausted, he paused to find himself resting on solid air.

Confused still, he brought his leg down several times to be met with resistance. There seemed to be dark strips lining this large box that contained a heavenly jungle, but the open spaces too were solid. When he peered down, he shuddered in shock. Another bee! Amazed and bewildered to see another of his kind led to this foul device, he cried for help, only to find the bee on the other side respond similarly.

In Beesdale's frustrated sigh a revelation came. In the corner of his vision, memory stood, growing from small containers of soil. The flowers. He knew his flowers, and he especially knew those flowers.

They were the same flowers from near his hive, the ones so violently uprooted as to eventually lead him here. In his current state, he questioned little, for he understood. Before him, inside this structure of solid air, was an alternate dimension, and he could only see himself in a utopia he would never be.

How selfish his other self was, as he complained about his standing, when he only needed to look around to see how lucky he was. The blind fool taunted Beesdale's hunger, never leaving his side from under the air. But Beesdale once more prevailed when he saw through this pseudo-reality back into his own. Beyond the invisible structure's walls were flowers freed from cursed vision.

Beesdale made haste, with trial and error, around his other self, who vanished as he parted ways with the unnatural solid air. An uneasy sense of terror stood in the back of his mind, for the flowers hid themselves away against a structure far bigger than the jungle before him, yet resembled so similarly his hive in perfectly grandiose construction. He pushed his fears aside and landed, tired and aching to feed.

He jumped flower to flower, each aroma different from the last, as he took in his fill. Well-rested he sat with contemplation, when another tune tickled his ear and captivated his senses. With fear consumed into courageous uncontrollable wonderment Beesdale launched himself away from the petal he rested upon.

With a gust of wind the small particles of pollen blew away seeking their destined homes. Upwardly moving, he found the sound louder, clearer, until witnessed a space of emptiness once more. He chanced it, and with great success zipped within confined surroundings.

Beesdale tried to move cautiously, but was too captivated by the sound. He drew nearer and nearer to the siren's call. Beesdale entered into the building through an opening in the wall and began to dance in the air, ignoring the strange two-legged giants, and their funny coverings, as they moved their hands over the silly objects they held.

He danced and swayed in tandem to the sounds he heard. Truly this was music. An experience never dabbled, Beesdale now took in more of this than any food or slumber he had before. He soared in great births as tiny eyes took in copious new sights.

Splashes of color off-set the solid white walls, as if creativity was crumbling the dull colors around him, shedding away the white and giving existence to myriad new worlds. Beesdale came dangerously close to collision with the strange concentration of hair upon the tops of their heads. Merely he made brisk flight, dragging clean-set strands asunder with his grooves. Sharply he turned upward, and spinning, came down. Beesdale's dance continued in loops, the room graced with a black and yellow blur, to compliment the statuesque titans' fastidious notes.

Suddenly the music stopped and a loud yelp disrupted that flowed grace upon the air.

"Why do you funny creatures with tufts of fur atop your heads stop? Do you not realize what a great and powerful gift you all possess?" As Beesdale questioned their actions his bee sense tingled, but by the time he reacted it was too late. He was suddenly struck with a blow thousands of times greater than any he ever experienced. Even the reprimanding blows of Beezy and H-Comb were a light breeze in comparison to the pain dished out by cruel giants.

Beesdale hit the ground with such force that he rebounded off the cold, hard surface of the giants' holding and rolled several times before coming to a stop. Disoriented, Beesdale frantically attempted to stand and escape, but his efforts were futile, for two of his legs were broken and one of his wings shredded to the point of uselessness. Attention was taken off his broken body when he was suddenly covered by large shadow. Looking up, he discovered the shadow came from one giant's foot.

Beesdale flailed two arms screaming, "Wait, stop! What was my crime!? Loving your beautiful music? Finding the sound of your mysterious objects to bring a soothing calm and joy? I beg of you, spare my life, I meant no harm to your kind!" But Beesdale's desperate cry for mercy could not be heard by the ominous colossus as his sole came down.

Beesdale, still alive but mortally wounded, lay next to the gray-green goo of his innards. Forced out of his body by the stomp, while his life blood slowly began to trickle out, like an hourglass signaling one's time is up. The fallen bee peered up, dazed, to see the titan smashing its palm against another's in celebration of taking down their prey. The enormous beings then sat back down and picked up their instruments once more.

Suddenly a fast paced tune began to emanate from their tools. It was Nikolai Rimsky-Korsakov's "The Flight of the Bumblebee." As Beesdale began his fade into unconsciousness he entered such a state of euphoria that he could actually see the notes shooting forth from the instruments; each set of notes a different color than the last.

In the middle of the song, all the notes of blue, yellow, green, purple, pale yellow, forest-green, light-violet, azure, lapis, and the like joined each other and formed a vibrant hive, far more glorious than the one Beesdale was born into, and sitting outside were other bees holding things similar to those of his executioners. They played fast, as quick as titans and faster still... Yet smaller, quieter. Around this vibrant hive was an enclosure of the finest and most unique greenery. A place free of banality, despite its peculiar familiarity.

As the song came to a close, the only thing left in his line of sight was the vibrant hive. All else was total darkness. Beesdale shed a tear, smiled and uttered softly, "My home, I'm going home..."

The Silk-Garbed Wolf

"See, I told you," Said Lou Pines, a partially Italian man with thick dark hair covering his head and face, beard and moustache whole. He threw a worn newspaper rifled with evident creases and curls on the table.

"Lou," his wife said pulling her hair back tightly above her soggy cereal bits, "We've been over this. I support you, I really do, but sometimes you have to be logical with your theories."

"You don't even know what it's about this time." Lou pointed to the article on page B8 of the local news.

"No need to show me. As sure as your back is hairy, you're on the werewolf idea again." His wife released her hair and clenched the spoon, as an ape, with three milk-soaked sugar bits.

"You know the dentist said you ought to cut back on your sugar."

His wife dropped the spoon, clanking against the bowl, milk droplets splattering the table's varnish. The steam of her coffee became the only subject of motion. A sudden twitch later, Lou's wife shoveled contents of the nearby sugar pot into her petite mouth, all of which was downed with a large sip of dissolved marshmallow bits. Lou reached out to grab her, but confusion gripped him to hesitation.

"Alright, don't blame me when your teeth wear away," Lou said defiantly. "Look at these canines, sharper and tougher than the day they grew in.

His wife chewed the remaining clumped sugar in her mouth. "Lishten, I know you upshet I dun't believe you, but ever shince kidsh left for shummer camp," she swallowed, "You had a lot of spare time. What I'm saying is, maybe you should focus on joining a charity or starting a hobby instead of jumping into the tabloid conspiracy trend."

"Don't give me that. I have plenty of hobbies! Just the other day I built that neat birdhouse," Lou said this as he waved his arm at the window behind him. He admired the elegance of his creation, a small, weakly supported box one might mistake as a birdhouse. However, there were extra pieces of wood attached and several nails jutted out. One could almost swear they heard that cheap, old wood creak and sway in the wind. A small finch flew by and landed, whereupon it hopped inside. Lou nodded to himself satisfied, when he witnessed a squirrel hanging from the branch above. It jumped to the birdhouse. Without warning the abode collapsed, a high-pitched chirp rang out nothing more. Lou gasped when he saw the poor squirrel drag itself away, back legs twitching. "Well uh, anyway, I'm not insane."

"Course not dear," She kissed his forehead lightly. "I've gotta get going, you think you'll make it to work okay?"

"Yeah, I'm getting a ride with Larry."

"Okay. And try not to fall asleep at work again, the last thing we need is to worry about how to pay the mortgage."

"Got my cup of coffee ready, maybe I'm addicted. Even though I've been sleeping so much more with the kids gone, I'm more tired than ever."

His wife was already by the door. "Make sure you also-"

"I know," Lou cut his wife off. "I'll call the bank about those mysterious charges." With that his wife was out the door. Lou rubbed his eyes and set to the task of scanning the daily newspaper for connecting evidence.

Half-an-hour later, Lou heard that distinctive clattering of Larry's truck, he folded his newspaper, now black, white, and highlighted yellow all over, and sauntered to the door. Lou saw Larry there with his hand raised in a ready tapping motion.

"Hey Lou, you ready?" Questioned Larry. "You don't look that great. Somebody punch you? Your eyes look all bruised."

"I'm fine. Let's just get going." Lou walked toward Larry's truck, but stopped by a certain tree in the yard. He shooed the birds away and pulled a different shoddily-built birdhouse off its rope and set it lightly, so very delicately, on the padded grass. Lou backed away carefully, ever so carefully, toward Larry's truck, when the birdhouse burst into flames.

"Wow, how'd that happen?"

"I'm not exactly sure," Lou sighed a mountain.

On the way to work, Lou and Larry discussed the matter on which Lou was stuck.

"Don't listen to the misses Lou," recommended Larry, his hands bouncing in the shaky truck. "I think you got a valid point, there ain't been no werewolf attack since I don't remember when. They can't really prove it ain't no shaggy beast."

"Exactly! Been reading through all the clippings I could find the past few months and everything falls together. Whoever finds a body mutilated beyond measure can't so much as even determine the gender of these victims, much less their identities. Happens about once a month, and it's always near the date of a full moon."

"There wasn't no slaying two months ago."

"Doesn't count, it was a cloudy night."

"Maybe, but don't you figure it's the energy of the moon does it? Don't figure clouds'd matter at all." Larry had a point, but Lou wouldn't be deterred from his beliefs.

"Whatever, I say it was cloudy, and it was cloudy. I got the weather reports right here."

"Cloudy maybe, and I ain't no scientist, but don't crazies get affected by a full no matter what?"

Lou let the possibility sink in. They hit a pothole which seemed to restart Lou's course of thought. "Anyway, they *almost* always happen on a full moon, and it's been a different spot each time, see? Always a shady, run-down motel, and who frequents these seedy motels? Cheap people sure, but who else? Prostitutes. I think this feller has a thing against street-walkers, gobbles them right up. Maybe he hates the values, maybe he gets a thrill from the hunt, or heck, maybe the guy has a nagging wife and accidentally kills the street-walkers when the feral parts kick in. No families, no trails. Get it?"

"Not sure if they're women though, judging by the papes you been reading," Larry said as he turned the wheel onto the last stretch to Lou's work. "Still, idea makes sense to me.

"Darn right it does, and my old lady thinks I'm nuts. All sorts of evidence, right here. Telling you, only some crazed animal could have done this, and no savage beast alone is renting rooms in a crowded city on someone else's dime. Don't make sense," Lou was on a roll now. "Besides, my old lady thinks I'm trying to fill some void with the kids at summer camp, but you and I both know I was working this long before that ever happened."

"Right? Must a started sometime after you got back from the doc. That strange bite wound ever heal?"

"Nah, still have the scar," Lou rolled his sleeve to reveal a large pink scar in the shape of an animal's maw. Despite Lou's hairy body, it stuck out bald. "Never could quite remember what happened on that hunting trip."

"You had a rough couple months. Don't let the misses get you down is what I say. Hey, why don't you come to the bar with me tonight?"

"I'd love to Lar, but I can't quit until I find the killer and prove werewolves really do exist. Plus I have to find a way to explain those motel charges, before my old lady nags on me again."

"Don't say you're keeping that up."

"But I was so close last time! I read the article on the recent murder. I was there in that very same motel, but I was too busy killing the roaches on the bathroom walls instead of paying attention like I should have. Even had the window open so the moon would signal me. Can't remember hearing a thing. Room must have been out of earshot. Maybe if someone tagged along..."

"C'mon Lou, I'm just a simple plumber," The truck *shunked* against another pothole, "A simple plumber adorned in my pale-blue jumper and greasy burgundy cap, which I always rub my palms on after oiling my tools. A kind of plumber that lives in his own humble way without sticking out too much. Surely I am the kind of man whose trade is demeaning but necessary, and that's who I am."

Lou raised his eyebrows surprised, "I'm shocked pal, I don't think I've ever heard you so poetic."

"Been practicin'. Reading a book called *A More Poetic Self in 14 Easy Steps: Plus the Chicks Dig it.* I'll lend it to you sometime."

"Good book?"

"Mmm."

Larry finally pulled into Lou's work, where Lou gripped the handle of the door which tore off. Lou stepped out flexing his bulbous muscles. "Sorry 'bout the handle. I been working out."

"Nice try. That handle been almost completely rusted off for weeks."

"Say Lar," Lou whispered as he drew close, "What do you figure I'm going to do? The danged werewolf hit every seedy motel in the city, a different one each murder, what if he don't attack again?"

"Doubt it."

"How do you mean?"

"I'm a plumber pal, I get around. Rumor has it the Full Moon Motel, located along Adwolf Road, went from two stars to one, making for the only seedy motel left not caught up in the bloodshed. Constructed back in 1978, it struggled to keep its quality up and the prices low. They ended up having to downsize, and after remodeling the rooms are so close together you can practically hear people breathing from any room, much less scream. And what with the cycle of the moon and all, seems like tonight is your werewolf's time to strike."

"Wow, thanks for the tip," Lou looked at his watch. "Gotta get in, must've hit too many red lights. Say you want a cup of coffee from inside before you get on?"

"Nah, I gotta get back to laying pipe."

"Got ya." Lou clacked his tongue and made his hand a gun-like shape.

"There *is something* you could do for me. My boss is riding with me later today, you mind holding my flask made of pure silver, so's I don't get trouble?"

Lou abandoned work. He had to plan; so he took the bus instead of waiting for Larry to show. He walked the rest of the mile from the bus stop to the Full Moon Motel. Lou had been there before, back when it was in better condition, for a little one night with his wife away from the kids. He perused the perimeter of the structure to see the various escape routes, and the best room to access the rest. Inside the lobby, if one bothered calling it so, Lou placed his charge card down on the desk and pointed out the window to the room specified. After a swipe and a sign, Lou was back on the street.

If Lou was to prove the theory claimed crazy, if Lou was to catch a killer, he'd need a witness to back his claims. As he walked the street thinking to himself, various people popped into his head. Larry was not a good option, he was busy trying to utilize the knowledge gained from his book. His wife thought he was going off the deep end, and she probably would have a pretty good case for adultery if she found he was renting rooms in seedy motel rooms every month. He tugged on his beard slightly, it always helped him think. The best option was an impartial stranger, but who would spend the night with an awkward scraggily man in a dark motel room? The thought finally exploded into his skull, the loose pieces expanding to the soft wall nearby. A stranger willing to spend the night in a run-down motel on the cheap, who else but...

Lou almost bumped her on the street. Before him a rather tall woman leaned against a streetlight with legs crossed, arms behind back, supporting her against the streetlight. The color of dying pumpkins dimly glowed on the woman's plump breasts almost overflowing from the silk tube-top suffocating two sizes too small. With an apparent dislike for twins, she also had a thing against small animals, because she wore an aged mink coat that also seemed not fit for her petite size. The tight clothing was to distract the faint marks on her face. Perhaps engaged in a few *disagreements* with unscrupulous folk, she had several small cuts to highlight her petite face. Not too noticeable to a common individual, Lou had been in his fair share of sharp scraps before. The streetlight mistress curled jet-black hair with her index finger. She had old-fashioned eighties big, wavy hair, but it was surprisingly attractive despite the long free-fall from style. Maybe it was the sweet scent in the air about her like ripe bananas, but it seemed the most perfect thing. He exchanged some words with no verbal return from the lone woman. It seemed her legs did the talking. He held out his hand, hers fell in. They were off.

In the motel, Lou doled out the reasonable, or so assumed cost, of the Lady of the Night's services. When Lou's hand dipped in pocket to return the faded leather of his aged wallet, he pulled out a black digital camera. He switched the camera on and a green light blinked, the lens pulled out with a whir, and he waited on the bed with his Lady of the Night. Lou noticed the tact of the place when the bed began to vibrate without coin. Lou kicked the snoring casket of failed marriage until it jerked and ceased. They sat for some time, Lou and his Lady of the Night, as they watched the sun further scale down the horizon. He tried to make small talk, but his Lady of the Night remained quiet and still. She would only pierce Lou's awed eyes, rub his leg off and on, and smile.

At the meeting of day and night, Lou's Lady of the Night opened the door and walked out. "Where are you going?" Lou stood holding tightly onto his camera. Not now, he couldn't lose his witness now. She made no answer. "Are you coming back? Please, come back soon!" She smirked faintly and waved her fingertips briskly. The air seemed to roll through her fingers, and they slid like smooth cream. Lou could almost taste it, with that scent in the air. She did not close the door behind her.

Lou sat on the bed fiddling with camera, taking distraction to see when his Lady of the Night would be back, and the situation of bright nightfall. He took snapshots to test the flash, and it burned quickly like a match. He started to grow excited, and soon tried to calm those nerves. He could not strand the post, the anticipation of the Lady of the Night's return his only hold.

He remembered in his pocket, Larry's flask. He unscrewed the metal cap and held that light pure silver body, where he tipped a small amount of warm liquid down. It quenched a parched throat against the moon's slow rise into night's sky. Suddenly Lou was wide-eyed and spat the remaining liquid to moldy carpet. He held back an alerted yelp. Stumbling to the bathroom clenching his mouth, he tore the faucet's handle off as cool, cool water streamed over his face. When Lou stared down the mirror, his mouth still smoked; a deep burn reddened and scarred where touched the flask. Hands too were lightly burned.

"What did that idiot pour in there, 180 proof?" Lou said trying to tend his wound. He expunged what he thought remained in his mouth. "Burned my mouth real bad. Hmm?"

Lou gazed to feel the full night sky, the moon fully past the horizon. Its glow stretched quickly over the land, until finally struck his crowded city. Soon its glow covered the Full Moon Motel, and through the windows and door the glow enveloped Lou Pines. He felt a sudden burbling inside, as all the bones in his body were shifting and stretching. His face felt incredible pressure as did a can in a compactor. Lou doubled over and tried to still his shaking body as it jutted various places that were soon sprouted more with hair. Instead of screaming pain, Lou howled.

Abruptly during such chain of events, the Lady of the Night returned, a bit bewildered, but none too scared. Her eyes drooped, and she giggled humbly when her one hand touch the other. Lou looked up at her as if he was begging her to save him. He reached his hand out, a hand that swelled and ruptured thicker, coarse fur, the color of midnight's dreary. The lightning adjustment sharpened fingernails into fine, hair-thin claws. His hand slammed back on the ground and his back stretched out thousands more miles than before, clothing tearing about his body as more shafts of hair shunted out. His burned mouth a hairless snout lined with saliva-dipped fangs that snapped and snarled, drool pouring out in each growl. Dark eyes slanted and gleamed brighter than the moon itself as a feral hunger set in.

Lou tried to warn her while still cognizant. Each month it happened, a loss of memory for a harvest night as the moon's light coated his skin, no matter how brief. And only when terrible transformation happened would realization come, a grand torture to hunt forever more, both as man, and wolf.

On all fours crouched to pounce, teeth clattered in anticipation of a monthly meal. He howled at the dazed Lady of the Night who simply stood with rather glazed, thin eyes as though she were sleepwalking. She positioned her arms to initiate a thin hug and smiled a likewise thin smile. No teeth shown, always those closed lips devoured in kindness.

Lou-turned-werewolf prepped the pounce but put leaned off-balance by burns on his front paws. His lunge shortened, but still reached enough in wolven hunger to tear amply through thick sheet-metal. The razor-sharp claws minced the wind ahead, almost splitting the atoms nearer him, his lust for food bringing close the neck of his prey.

A loud dog's yelp was later reported by peoples on the streets of the noisy city. Inside the Full Moon Motel, hanging from various prickly spears, as cattle on meat-hooks, was the body of Werewolf Lou. He grimaced, exhausted into the wider grin of the Lady of the Night. The grin seemed to circumnavigate jaw, and when wider opened her narrow eyes, six other faint cuts on forehead cracked open to reveal more eyes. The legs sprouted from bushels of brown-spotted hair matted to her back. No fur coat after all. Werewolf Lou attempted to free himself by shifting free weight against the legs, but was locked in tight. Puddles of blood poured to the ground, and he grew too weak to further resist.

The Lady of the Night's thumbs slipped gently into her skin-tight shorts, which outline *everything*, slender hips rocked back and forth as she slipped them off ever-so-slowly. She slid her moist pink tongue over her lips passionately and bit gently into Werewolf Lou's hairless snout. He no longer felt the pain, but was now completely immobile. As her tight, skimpy panties slinked to the ground in a heap with her pants, her bare skin showed through, but these were no regular ladies' parts. A clump of hair around her crotch, very 70's, unwound into a bulbous tip behind her. She petted the coarse fur of Werewolf Lou, now sticky in oogey ooze, for a moment and then placed him lightly on the ground, the four prickly legs slipping out with a *shluck*. The legs shuddered and bodily juices splattered the walls and the floor and even the ceiling. As she squatted, a leg reached back and closed the door behind her, smearing brush strokes of Werewolf Lou's squishy insides and shedded hair.

Her approach clicked Werewolf Lou's memory. He had seen this woman prior, and now he placed it. She glided by his window last month while he waited intently in the motel. She seemed so calm and vacant-eyed back then too.

She fidgeted and crawled about like a tailor on an exquisite suit. Werewolf Lou was breathing shortly and could not make out her actions, yet every now and then he saw strands of white fluid pouring onto him; a tight pressure grew and constricted his lungs. Instants later the bulbous tip pointed toward his face, the white fluid blasting onto his snout and oozing into the maw. His fangs felt the sticky nature of it, and the great distaste, like bitter apples.

The Lady of the Night grabbed one loose strand attached to Werewolf Lou and dragged him to the closet, a prickly leg pulling the door open. She supported his body and tied the strand snug to the pole inside. He hung there suspended, tilting back and forth minutely, whereupon he came face to face with a similar worried expression also covered in white fluid. His eyes bulged like seeded grapes, and he tried to rock himself free, to no avail. His skin was a tinge blue, no doubt from circulation loss, all Werewolf Lou could make out before the four prickly legs squeezed around the man inside and ripped him out. He screamed a muffled cry, but even the heightened senses of a werewolf barely made it out through the sticky stuff.

Her lengthy grin popped open and was given wide berth. Fangs stood in various spots like jagged glass in a broken window. Her wide crevasse continued to gain space until her skin seemed to split and crack open; her mouth was a seething cavernous hole ready to suck the man down. She slowly lowered agape, her shadow swallowing whole the worried man first, as he started to vibrate as the bed had done. Perhaps that was how she liked them best, salty with cold sweat outside, warmer fluids to follow up. As she kept her mouth stretching, it seemed to shudder at its limits. The man's scream echoed within the cave, now a third of the way in.

With a quick snap the glass fragments clamped down, and he squirted like an overfilled éclair. As she sunk deeply in, she rubbed her jaw back and forth to saw the bone away, yellowish fatty lipids seeped out through the punctured wounds as the man ripped into pieces like quality jerky. The yellowish lipids made the snack greasy, the crimson blood gushed into her mouth and spilled profusely down her chin onto her supple breasts and over her quivering legs. It made a small kiddy pool with all the types of smelly liquids staining the old, moldy carpet.

A starved eater was the Lady of the Night, as she crunched the bones to fine powder in her mouth, still open, drool dripping down like sap because of the man's stable spinal column. With various twists and jerks she finally snapped the vertebrae off. She slurped and munched with massive gibbering jowls that flapped as her teeth crunched together.

Every now and then she would suck delicately on the body, without taking a bite, scraping lightly into the skin to stray any chance of clotting. Though wrapped tightly in a sack of white fluid, it was sticky, and stuck to the man's frame as it was, Werewolf Lou could see the man of average build collapsing inward. Sucked dry, like an exhausted balloon, wrinkles on bones prodding the outline.

It seemed like hours of feasting, but the coming fall allowed for few moments of darkness, so it may not have been more than 30 or 45 minutes. Every now and then a nerve would be jabbed by a fang and the sack would wiggle through the stages of rigor mortis. The Lady of the Night raised the body and shook it, her massive jowls inflating and deflating as she shrieked in a high-pitched skittering sound. The body dropped and the Lady of the Night, now of red skin, wiped her mouth clean with the prickly legs that seemed to dance and sway about the air in delight.

She walked a sexy model's walk, left leg over right, as though it were the most natural thing to do at the time. She paused in front of Werewolf Lou hanging upside-down, his eyes feral still, but animal spirit tame. She placed her hand lightly on her naked belly, plump and round against the rest of appearance. A prickly leg brushed Werewolf Lou's face in brief circles while she stared with that usual smirk. Another leg reached for the closet's handle. The door shut tight.

My Wife's Cute Killing Device

I knew she was going to one day, just not so soon. Maybe in my mid-forties, sure, but I'm still at least eight years off from that. She bought it anyway, behind my back. Aren't all the methods of untimely death done in such a matter? I don't know why it has to happen this way. I thought I was a good husband. Sure, I sleep a lot, and I watch the occasional television, but I work all day darn it!

I remember seeing it for the first time and fearing for my life. It was hidden in the closet, laid down on some blankets. I backed up, horrified, and starting thinking about my last will and testament. She started getting lazy with the thing though, roaming about with it and placing it on the bed or kitchen floor.

I feel like I can hear it now, that subtle rumbling, an earthquake coming to take me down to Hades. Like a smooth engine running on golden oils, that's the sound. I peak down and see the thing squinting at me with those glowing slits for eyes. It sees me and it knows. I shut my eyes tight and pretend to sleep until I do.

It is the next day, getting ready for work, she's staying home today. Hopes to get some "chores" done. I have to loosen this tie. I see it out of the corner of my eye, following me, that engine sound always signals the approach. I grab my coffee cautiously. Keep the mind of a lion-tamer, show no fear. I grab my cup and the newspaper as best as I can with the briefcase and I stumble as I turn around. The coffee spills to the ground and I curse. The thing had wrapped itself around my legs while I held scalding coffee. Luckily the coffee mug was the only thing that spilled to the tile-laden floor, but I could be next easily enough.

I try to kick it, but she grabs him up and scolds me. Me the one who was almost slain! She cuddles the demonic thing and rubs the bristly fur as that engine revs up to mock me. It won the round, but I the battle, alive enough to work, which may not have been much at all. Lucky thing, protected by her arms. Holding so tight onto the fuzzy thing as it whips its tail at me in a secret attack.

After work I relax a bit with a stiff drink. She hates it when I drink, but then again, I hate it when she tries to kill me, so I suppose we're even. She tells me of her day through gritted teeth avoiding my amber-filled glass. On she goes about how she cleaned the tile, paid the bills, and almost managed to get most of the laundry done. Then I guess she fine tuned her death machine, flailing my old socks as it jumped around and pounced, gaining my scent to hone in on my weakest moment.

I grow tiresome of her talking at me, so I make a move for the kitchen to cook up a simple dinner, grilled cheese and tomato soup. As I'm going, however, I see a flash of black shoot out from under my chair and into the path of my next step. I, despite hating the devil, try to move out of its way before landing, but it looks up with wide eyes and predicts my movement. Its tail fully stepped on, me dropping my good liquor glass.

It didn't splinter all over the place, the glass broke into several large chunks, but it ruined thoroughly. She stands there caressing the thing she brought to do me in. She's yelling that I should be careful, that I'm only thinking of myself, but I'm wise to her. She wants me gone, to off me, drop my body in a dumpster for all she cares. Wants to be free and have all my stuff, but I don't think so. I'll find a way to dispose of the thing without her knowledge.

I am ready for bed now. Hair prickles on my neck as I hear it behind me scratching at loose pebbles. I try to ignore it, but it is scratching at my brain, destroying my mind to make the kill that much more enjoyable. Or maybe the thing is playing with me, like all their kind do before the end.

I pull on my pajamas and stretch to ready for a slumber most pleasant, for only in my dreams do I find peace from the thing. As I pull back covers to join her in bed, she tells me she almost forgot about the last load of laundry. She asks so politely and in such a nice manner, I feel a great obligation. Here I thought it was the victim of the executioner who got the last request.

I lift the heavy load up into my arms, the thing is easily piled over and almost tipping from all the fabric, and by the looks of it, they all belong to her. I walk to the steps and notice the lights out downstairs. It is a difficult traverse not to see the steps below, much less farther ahead. And yet, there in the darkness with this large basket do I hear my wife's cute killing device hidden there in the shadows. I take the first step down with feather-footed caution and hear the creak echo down the stairwell, covering over that smooth engine.

The sounds battle with each other to take the precedence in my mind. Each slow hum is danger and each loud creak is my friend. Only fourteen steps to go...

Crash Course 101

"You've always hated Mother," said Connie. There she was, raking away at the self-esteem of David again. A cavernous pit already, she always found some dirt down there.

"I don't hate your mother. I don't feel like talking to her every moment we're there is all." David gripped the wheel tightly. They had been over the fiasco for almost an hour, and he was starting to get desperate in the most obscene ways. He started to pray. Maybe an owl picked up a stray gun, gleaming under the moonlight, and would drop it to the solid asphalt. Loose grip, old owl, and then bang, a stray shot kills him. Or maybe he could swerve off the road and slam into a tree hard enough to do him in.

Still too cowardly to pull it off. That was how he ended up getting married to Connie. She was not a first choice by any means, but David did not want to be alone for the rest of his life. He did not see himself as any great sturgeon to Hiawatha either. So there he was taking Connie's delirious bullshit again. Usually she was not so bad, but David stayed quiet at home just the same, if but to at least stave off the fire-stoked coal inside her.

The car throttled and lost its rev. David kicked down the accelerator several and it kicked back in, thrusting its two passengers tight against their seat. There was a slight rumble humming in the engine. The rumble reignited Connie too, "Oh, the transmission was fixed he said, trustworthy salvage yard this time he said, last another couple of months at least he said."

"Listen Connie, *dear*, I told you I would have it looked at when we had the money."

"You would have more money if only you would have taken my father's offer for a job, but not you. Not Mr. Independent. Not Mr. I'll-do-it-myself. Now look where I am. A shaky car about to die in the middle of goddamned Sleepy Hollow."

"Hold on, what offer? Your father is unemployed!"

"Oh I see, now my father is a lazy lout. Sorry my family doesn't come from the same standards as your family. Screw you," Connie turned away begrudgingly. David wanted to say something, but all he could do was sit in shock from what he heard, his hand, palm upward in the *What the Hell* fashion. The trees seemed ever more attractive, but he kept his hands steady, he was not ready to water those roots with his mortal coil yet. This too would come to pass.

Connie did prove an interesting point though. A point which David tried to focus on to quell his irate fog. And in the tense silence the main point was clear to him. Screw Connie's mother. Fuck her and her whole stable. Connie got on his nerves too. Sometimes he wanted to bash her thick head in. He was sorry for that thought, he didn't really mean it. A slight hiss could be heard pouring from under the hood. The radiator.

They had to make it to at least the next well-lit city. That light would extinguish his darkness, but that was at least twenty miles away. The car reacted the same way it did before, David gripped even tighter to the wheel. Those tricky trees were tough-skinned, but less cold than his passenger. He wanted a stick-shift, but Connie refused to learn. Said it was too hard in rush hour. So there they were driving an automatic, black Beretta, its digital display clicking back and forth to adjust to the changing speeds, all the meters checking out around halfway. At least he could pretend he was piloting KnightRider. Yes, the Hoff. And so it was the real value of the car to him revealed: make-believe. Maybe the main function was taken to greater levels than David wanted. Probably explained Connie too.

Still, David was in little mood, and with the only light on the road emanating from the Beretta's weak headlights, Mr. Sandman's grip grew tighter. While Connie fumed in quiet, David was unconcerned with the difficulties of marriage. One day she would be better, but then, as his friend had always told him time and again, "Dude, women are crazy, that's just how it is."

David had the briefest moments, mere milliseconds, where he fell to sleep, eyelids sealing and arms falling limp against the wheel, as does a soulless corpse. As soon as his head dipped in any fashion, however, he bobbed into awareness, wide-eyed and bewildered. "Connie. Connie. Um, Connie?" No use. No response. No effort to turn and unclamp her welded, rusty arms. David was condemned to more driving, hands attached to the wheel, a regular Johnny Tremain. He slapped himself lightly so as to not draw attention to his condition, but the string of actions repeated itself with strengthened severity.

On the seventeenth bob, David rose to awareness once more and saw rapidly moving toward them, or rather the Beretta toward it, a large cat. As they drew closer, as though in slow motion, David found not a cat, but the most hideously large white rat. The creature changed shapes once more and became what it actually was, a hungry possum. The possum made no attempts to move, despite the harsh change in light that grew brighter with each passing fragment of a second. It chewed delicately in the middle of that road, hunger overtaking its fight-or-flight reactions.

David, being a man not of the sort to purposely strike animals, swerved one way and when the oaken bark was to halt the car, David swerved back the other way, bending around the uncaring possum with its shrewd face and yellowed fangs gnawing on some greasy edible substance. Connie slid into David, grabbing tightly to the passenger door, and started yelling at him to slow the car down, to slow the car down and brake. She smacked him on the arm like he was some brute. It didn't help David regain control. As he was pulling himself back to his lane

with a third swerve, the car a sidewinder in smooth sand, turned
back the way it was headed, off-road, and another larger creature
came into view.

Once more David had full view of everything for so long,
but his capability for heightened reaction was already expended
into getting full use of the road. His hands on the wheel could
not convince the car to change its course. Into the light
illuminated was the back of a man, laden in simple plaid and
jeans, an average sort wearing a hefty cap. The man seemed to
hold his steps and turn, his shoes now reflecting as to say, "Don't
hit this pedestrian!" They were covered in revealing dry, crusted
mud around the lower perimeter. His eyes grew wide, the pupils
paralyzed at their fullest. David kicked down the emergency
brake and slammed his other foot down upon the brake pedal.
The car squealed and churned and chunked, but in the end was
not enough. As the man turned fully around, the car struck him
head on, his body launched backward. The car followed
hungrily. The grinding sound ceased only when the car finally
came its slowest roll, a small lump and another crunch held the
car at its stop.

The car rattled and sputtered as David almost squeezed
through the thick material of the steering wheel, white-knuckled
and huffing heavy, David's hand shook as it slowly reached for
keys and put the bloodthirsty machine to sleep. He stared there,
in the darkness, in the awe of the action he had wrought upon the
two of them.

Connie finally spoke up, absent-minded, in equalized
shock, "W-What just happened?" She turned slowly to look
deeply into David's eyes with worry. Surely her anger had
passed and new resolve entered her life, or so David thought.
"What did you do?"

David sat there, motionless, contemplating those
consequences. "David, David! C'mon you lout, snap out of it.
We have to do something." David looked slowly over at her and
nodded. He left the car's engine off, and his fingers lightly
missed the attempt at the hazard lights as they frisked with lacked

ample force. David seemed not to notice such frivolities. The door slammed shut behind him.

They approached the man cautiously, Connie checked his pulse, "He won't last long, that's for sure. Great driving David."

"There was a possum in the road," David said with a low hanging head. He crouched beside the man.

"Leave it to you to save a disgustingly ugly animal by killing a man."

"It isn't my fault! He wasn't all the way off the road." Connie kept fixed on the man. "C'mon look! Look how much of the Beretta is still out on the road. Look!"

"Oh David, stop being so pathetic. You can make excuses for anything can't you?" Connie sighed. David could see her forehead was scrunching together again. "We have to do the only thing that makes sense."

"You're right dear, as always."

Connie looked up sharply, "And what does that mean?"

"Nothing, I'm saying you know best."

"I know you, you wily little sniveler. You're implying I am responsible for you hitting this innocent soul."

"What? No, I-"

"Whatever. Is that a gas can?" It certainly was. Plum empty, drier than the Sahara. David realized the man must have been hoofing it for gas, but he did not recall seeing any cars on the side of the road. Maybe he passed it during one of the moments he nodded off. Something had to be done.

"We have to drive back." Connie stared at David as if he presented the craziest of ideas. As if David had said they needed to attach straws to a glass of rocks to build a helicopter. "I'm serious Connie, we *have* to. What if there is somebody waiting for him in a car back there, and that person waits, and waits, and waits, but this guy never comes back? Oh Jesus, what if this guy had his wife and kids singing campfire songs until they could rush to window screaming, 'Daddy Daddy.' Oh damn, damn! We gotta fess up Connie, we done something awful terrible. Tell the family, help out. Yes, maybe that can redeem us."

Connie sat in silence as she rolled the thought around in her head. "Not me."

"Wait, what?"

"Not me. *I* didn't kill him. *You* killed him. There's no blood on my hands. To think I would marry a murderer. Father always said there was something about you. Never would have thought it would be your thirst for blood."

"Stop it Connie, shut up!"

"What did you say to me?" She flicked him a cold stare as her forehead eroded from cracked sidewalk to deeply gorged canyons. David silenced. "Later David, *later*. We have to act quickly. This road might not be vacant long. Never know when we'll see the next set of headlights, and it's hard to explain away a dead body in the middle of nowhere as an old chum who just happened to drop dead because it was such a perfectly starry night. Get in the car."

"You mean just leave him here? No! He might still have a chance." David picked the man's arm up and dropped it. It fell like a sack of potatoes or perhaps even rocks. He flinched slightly and looked at Connie. "We can't just leave the body here, it's wrong."

"Lottery's over David, he lost. You should have thought about rights and wrongs before you hit him!" David felt growing warmth from Connie constantly rubbing it in. She could see she was about to break him and pulled her final card. "Fine, whatever. You go ahead and dilly dally. I'm waiting in the car. I have to perfect the look if someone comes while you're dragging the thing here and there."

Connie started to saunter back to the car with her head held high. David quivered and stared at the peacefully still body. He steadied himself and took a deep breath. His chest out, he grabbed a hold of the man's arm and part of his vest. When he got the body partially off the ground, he faintly witnessed tiny bugs swimming in feast-full pleasure in the sticky stuff the leaked under the man. He lost his grip when his stomach gripped him. The man suspended partially in the air by a vest with threads that were loose at the seams. The front portion of the vest became thread-bare as the body fell to the ground in a thump, an ant or two blasting away in the wind. He tried not to look, but he had to get the body out of the ditch, or road, it was hard to tell where the man lay precisely.

A bare chest splattered and torn much like the vest where lay a pattern of gore. The flytrap. Not even Connie was going to resist the plan once she stepped near the sticky strip. He signaled her over, and with enough convincing, came. She looked but could not quite make out what David spoke of, but the illumination of his cell phone made it clear. Carved deep into the man's chest was the discernable image of license plate numbers. Connie denied it at first in disbelief of the predicament, but the three set letters and likewise three numbers after matched the plate on the Beretta. Additionally, the vest may have soaked up any excess blood, for the imprint was solid and clear. David did not think he had hit him so high, but he was not thinking quite clearly during the incident.

Connie bent down and massaged the air above the wound as if to see it a figment of her imagination. Touch would make reality. Clear as night could provide the wound's red lines perfectly outlining the indentations, upon what seemed to be some support structure for it beneath a bed of shattered ribs. Must have been how the man died, punctured lungs. His last breath leading two non-suspect killers to guilt. David really hated visiting his mother-in-law.

Connie stood and shook her head. "Now we have to take the sap with us. Had to get a good hit in didn't you David? Leave your mark? Make sure he never had a fighting chance?"

"What! But I-"

"David, please, not now. Help me lift the body."

David held back his retorts and got a better glance at the road. He shakily looked for some length, to check for coming headlights, but instead found clarity of shadowed road, no possum in sight. David nodded, "Right. To the backseat?"

"Of course not. The trunk. Less suspicious and much easier to clean."

"Give the man some respect."

"Listen *dear*, I just vacuumed those seats. You might not care about staining the backseat, but what about when I go to the dry cleaners? You can't always be so selfish. Now lift, you're barely pulling your weight. What a waste of a gym membership."

"Sorry honey." David clicked the trunk open while balancing the man's body, his legs limp and bent uneasily the wrong way. David had noticed the car crunched over something. Poor guy looked like a teddy bear that lost its stuffing in the left leg, all flat and pathetic-like. David abruptly dropped his end of the body and the man almost collapsed onto Connie. She shot him the look and David wondered what was left for her forehead to wrinkle, resourceful woman. But then again David was used to her talents because he woke up to that look almost every day for at least the past six months. He tried to appeal to her course of reason, "I don't think the trunk is such a good idea Connie, I mean, we have our suitcase back there. And that is fine, luxury travel casing my dear."

Connie was not so foolish as to take bait with no worm, "What a better resting place and means of travel. Indonesian children could only wish they were lucky enough." She could see his moral territories grew larger the farther they went, but she was not the type to not get what she felt she deserved. "Or maybe you'd rather take the emergency knife out of the trunk and cut the plate number out of the sap's skin. We can dispose of that somewhere else."

"You mean that small pocket knife with the nail file, toothpick, and crappy scissors?"

"Don't look at me dearest, I'm holding the body. You're the only one who can do it. I'm quite squeamish about the whole ordeal, but I'm stronger headed than you. Now get to cutting, because I'm not leaving any evidence for the cops to come knocking at my door four days from now at the ungodly hours of the early morning. I do have work you know."

David had no idea where the little red pocketknife was, much less how to go about the procedure. The knife was barely sharp enough to wedge through melted butter. He thought to himself, *if only I could find a big enough rock*. What was he saying? Thinking about grinding against the bony soup-bowl with a weighty rock until the skin had scraped away. It almost made David lose it, and the bile was already built up near the top of his throat, ready to release. He sighed, shamed, and clenched his fists. He did so until fingernails dug deeply into his own moist flesh. How disgusting even then. He clenched the man's free arm and nodded to Connie, "In the trunk then?"

They closed the trunk together, but were met resistance with a certain crunch sound, like biting into burnt toast. The wobbly leg was not shoved in correctly. David cringed and his cheeks puffed, but he swallowed his bitter stomach brew. He didn't need Connie complaining about paint next. They slammed the trunk again. It stayed shut and sealed.

David noted the hazard lights not flashing, wondering if the battery had died. He hoped against it, yet he did not recall actively striking the button in the first place. The driver and passenger doors closed simultaneously, David adjusted himself in the driver's seat, the button near the wheel not depressed. That thought gave him a little deserved relief as he reached for the keys in the ignition, Connie silent but aggravated, and he turned the keys, driving off.

Or So David had hoped. As soon as the key turned, a spark shrieked through the engine to the starter which pulled and whirled its metal parts, the rest of the engine revved up. The car remained still, but ran smoothly. David cupped his hand around the automatic shift-stick and pulled it down to drive. The car started to roll forward slowly, and his foot pressured the accelerator. As soon as it pushed, a loud chunk laughed and the car smiled forward one last time. David kept kicking down the pedal, and the engine roared like a sleepy lion without. The car made no attempts at movement. RPM shot up like a junkie in a needle factory. David pounded his hand on the steering wheel and almost began to cry.

"Great going idiot! You ruined the damned car, right when we were so close!"

"N-No Connie, it's nothing, don't get upset. I'll go fix it right now." David reached down and released the hood. He turned the car off once more. He slid the keys into his pockets toughly, almost tearing through the cheap fabric of his pants. He smiled fake hope at Connie who sat inside with stone face and iron-clad, folded arms. She looked like an out-of-shape, female version of those guardian statues emperor Qin had protecting his afterlife. He waved a limp-wrist at her outside as he raised the black Beretta's hood. He pulled out his cell phone for light and inspected the car.

David had no idea why he bothered. His knowledge of cars was limited to a simple oil change, and maybe a headlight fix, but this sounded a lot worse. He knew deep down what it was, anyone even remotely familiar with automobiles would. It was the transmission.

It had finally given up when all transmissions are destined to, at the absolute worst possible time. In David's case, when he had a dead body stuck in the trunk. Of course it had to be when there was a dead body in his car, it was like the transmission could smell it, sense when it was needed most, and taking the mantle of the Schmoo, killed itself for the feast of parts dealers. All David wanted was a hot cup of coffee and an out-of-the-way makeshift graveyard. Instead David fiddled around with various nonsensical items compared to the problem at hand: checking the oil, looking at the battery connection, and making sure the windshield washer fluid was topped off. He had to look busy while he thought up an excuse to feed Connie. Yes food, she would definitely go for that.

And of course the old saying, "Speak of the Devil and he shall come," had to happen, because David heard, rather felt, vibration of the passenger door throughout the entire body of the

Beretta. The sounds of dry footsteps over soft dirt as Connie emerged from behind the hood. She placed her hand around the side of the hood for support as she stood there, eyes squinted.

"What's taking you so long?"

"Nothing, nothing. Looking around is all." David reached for a random dipstick and pulled it out. "Oil is a little low."

"That's the transmission, dipstick. God, don't you know anything, the oil is over there. Did you let the transmission fluid get low? No wonder the thing broke down! Metal against metal. The car is a lot like you David. Move." Connie pushed David aside as she leaned over the engine and fiddled around. Even in the dark she seemed to know what she was doing. She reached further down and felt around. "Nothing else wrong. Just like I figured, I'm going to jail because my fool of a husband dropped the tranny. Oh God, I've already wasted my life for the past couple years, why do I have to rot away in an orange jumpsuit too?"

"Hey now, we can figure something out."

"Why don't you think? Why didn't you consider the car might need a check-up? But not you Mr. Busybody, no no. Not you. You might be a depressing little prick, but don't take your one-and-only down with you!" Connie was yelling, fuming at David, but she never turned around, kept fiddling with the car like some spider-monkey mechanic.

"But Connie, you don't understand. It isn't-"

"No! You listen to me. You're so selfish, thinking you do so much and me so little."

"Please listen to-"

"Oh I'll get it fixed this weekend. Your life is a mess and you're making me a slob just the same. You know how many times I could have left you but didn't? Maybe I should have. Maybe have one more working car and one less dead guy in the damned trunk. And another thing-"

David threw his hands down in frustration, he was yelling now, yelling back, "Just listen! You have to-"

"How dare you interrupt me!" Connie wobbled as she delved deeper in that engine, small clinks echoing out under the silence of passed screams. "I don't hate you David, but Mother was right. David the dummy, that's what she called you at first, before she grew fond. Turns out she was right all along. David the dummy, the big wooden fool."

David tried to release. He stepped back further in a defensive stance and was ready to explode. David was not the sort to get angry. He was the kind of guy who got pushed and stayed there. The kind of guy who, when pushed against that wall, would buy the guy a drink. But once he was pushed through the drywall of his lengthy, patient calm, David entered into a dark room that scared him. No light bulbs in reach. He wanted out. There were howls in his head blocking his rational thought in the darkness, and he clambered for the light through the hole, but Connie kept kicking him back in. The wolves of his lamb mind drew near.

He held tight to his fingers. The pressure in the radiator was growing, he wanted to warn Connie, but she did not want to listen. The pressure expanded vastly and more compressed in the small shape. All that steam and hot breath had to be released. It kept inside, all of it. The cap was loose, and the head of the thing was growing red with primal rage.

Finally the cap popped straight off and the steam blew everywhere. In the fog David could not see, it seemed instinct to knock off the hood's support rod and bring it down. Not enough, too much pressure still. David kept the hood aloft. He brought it down hard as he had the trunk. Connie muffled yelps; legs spasm as her body see-sawed with each drop of the hood. He kept going long after the repetitive thud and after his arms grew tired from the hood's weight. Only when the hiss started to subside throughout the forest did his mechanical actions cease.

David's body shook and teeth rattled as if very cold. He stepped away, the hot steam gone. Not a drop of water present. He wondered in disbelief his eloquent execution. "Connie? Connie? Connie, dear? Dear lovely, come, time to get up." She did not move. She just laid there. And she said he was the lazy one, back to sleep again, while David stayed awake. Rude of her, but okay. She could sleep for now, no matter of how tired he became. When David's hand patted the hood of the car, the fog had finally cleared and into his mind, clarity free from bitching. With renewed sense of silence, thoughts of every nature rushed through his mind. Airy regret, soggy remorse, wooden satisfaction, fiery fear. Surely the act of the ghostly Connie whom would haunt him even beyond the mortal coil. *'Till death do them part indeed.*

David shuffled to the car and fidgeted with the handle until it threw open. He jumped in, door following shortly behind. Sitting there in the quiet the whispered voices within him yammered still, safe from the ghostly presence of Connie. Her body was gone from view, instead a horizon of raised black metal. David gripped the steering wheel and felt its vinyl deep in the creases of his hands as he rubbed. He clunked his head lightly upon that same wheel, and he wept. So empty within for so long, beaten down, but perhaps now with her gone, he remembered only good times when she and he were more rambunctious.

The intense loss within him turned the key within. Moving not, the spark fired through his body to the conscience, its concepts and morals whirred and clicked as it roared through his active mind. The car broken and stranded, but the mind purring, he was ambushed by an army of invaders invisible to his eye. He did what he needed to do.

He wept. He wept hard. And as tears streamed down his face, the shadows of the forest overlapped all potential for light that shone through. Still, the light would not be ignored. David noticed the soft yellow slowly filling the black Beretta. Dumbfounded by such illuminations, it seemed to blind him for his ignorance. Squinting hard, David saw two raging sunbursts advancing to consume him, it screeched through his delicate eardrums and roared through his rotten belly.

Several cans crunched near an amplifier and David gained a newfound power. The essence of time seemed to retard as glass dust glittered confetti from the monster with sunburst eyes. David took flight at once, the cost of which a headache to split an oak, but such were the consequences of unwavering concentration. His hope dashed far from him when witnessed the forgotten Connie's limp legs. They dragged along trying to follow, whereupon fear and guilt blew out candle's troubled escape. The light failed him, but he finally felt what it was to fly free among the stars, weightless. But David had to join his departed beloved and so did when the ball and chain relocked tightly about him. He dived down, bound to the earthly root nearby dear Connie

A hefty door opened and a frail woman poured out, laden with tears. A man opposite her fell onto the ground and shook himself to proper awareness. They gathered themselves together and glanced over the wreck.

"I let you drive my car once and you crash it! Oh man, my ride." The man rubbed his forehead and kicked the air wildly.

"I'm sorry. I'm so sorry! I didn't even see the car; it was like it was invisible."

"Gosh," The man cricked his neck, "What jerk parked this thing halfway in the middle of the road?"

They made their way to the front of the car and saw the shattered windshield, the rest of the mess out front. Loosely dangled legs from under a hood and a man with deep gashes through head and face most thoroughly, constricted and solid, as though choked by something.

"Jesus!" The man jumped back. He looked worried for a moment and set his eyes on the girl. "Why'd ya have to hit them! I told you to drive careful, I told you!"

"It isn't my fault, honest. I didn't mean to." She tugged her long hair tightly around her head for comfort. "Let's get the police, they can help."

"The police? Are you crazy? We ain't going to jail babe."

"It was an accident. They'll understand, they have to."

"Sorry babe, sounds like clear manslaughter. That's more time than I'm willing to take. We just drive home like it never happened."

"We can't just leave their bodies," the woman flicked her hand as to display the gory scene. "Look at them. Look at the dedication this couple had. The wife must have been looking at the engine while her husband kept his eye on the dash, and we done them in."

"Whoa babe. We? *You* killed them, I was just keeping an eye on the ride. I messed up. Let a woman drive, big mistake. Let's go, we can't worry about them."

"But-"

"Now!"

They made haste to the car, but then a flytrap never is never enough. A rattrap clamped tightly where the sticky failed. They saw there in the shadowed iridescence from within crushed metal. Overlaying the hood was a fine coat of blood as though squished out of a ketchup packet. They looked at each other and realized they gobbled that cheese too soon. Even if they managed to get back with their damaged car and deathbed engine, surely they could not explain away the exact correlation of their front end to the back of this black Beretta. Surely the police would connect it. And the wash of crimson red over their hood would not aid in lessening the suspicions of the town folk some miles ahead.

"We have to grab the bodies. Help me out here." The man ran toward the front of the Beretta.

"What are you talking about? We'll never be able to dispose of all the evidence. We have to fess up," She pleaded to no avail.

"Shut up and be useful for a change. Sometimes I wonder why I ever walked out of the bar with you." She walked over and grabbed David's body, but had trouble pulling it. He snipped, "Lift! You're not lifting!"

"Stop yelling at me."

"I wouldn't have to yell if you'd just lift!"

As they drug the body closer to their car, the girl got a closer look at their newly damaged vehicle. The blood almost seemed to be cooking into the paint of the car with the smoky air. The radiator was steaming and boiling inside; a cap rattled loosely around.

Jumpin' Jupiter

Must have been the summer of forty-six when it happened. Now I'm not going to lie to you and say we were really prepared. We didn't have the ability to intercept them. No flying cars or personal space satellites like those movies of the future my grandfather always used to watch. Kind of boring actually, aside from some higher taxes, and Hostess still made delicious baked goods for mass-manufacturing.

So we pretty much had to sit and wait. Plenty awareness of what was to come, had the most up-to-date communications systems in the world, but no way to intercept or stop their arrivals.

I myself was drafted one year prior to the invasion. I was kind of scared at first, because of the tension between us and Russia. Used to remember my grandfather telling me about the Cold War. Funny how history seemed to repeat itself. When we heard that our real enemies were from Jupiter, we were more confused than anything else. We didn't really know what their beef with us was. Deep down though, we expected it would be something like this.

It must have been almost 15 years since the last invasion. Not by the Jupitarians of course, that would have been silly. It was the folks from Pluto that time around. They had finally gotten word people were saying they weren't a planet, but rather a stranded moon. Guess they thought we were going to kick

them out of the solar system or something, like we had the
authority.

 I remembered the panic well. They tried to keep it a
secret for so long, but eventually the government fouled up when
some hot shot reporter somehow leaked the secret. The reporter
died of an abrupt heart attack shortly thereafter, despite peak
physical condition. The government kept trying to tell us it was
all a hoax, but it was too late. The snowball had already rolled
too far down the hill to stop. People were in a terrible fuss over
the whole thing. First the public started going into a buying
frenzy, the man with the money won out, but when supplies grew
dim, the strongest fist seized the torch. Big cities everywhere
were on fire. Luckily, I was in a small town, so I didn't get
involved in most of the rioting. Amazing how, when pressured,
my own honest neighbors turned into common thugs. They
borrowed from my grandfather until we had nothing left to give.
Even that was barely enough to appease them. Those scattered
gun-happy cops sure did have a hey-day. They itched their
trigger fingers raw.

 I was a young lad at the time and I thought it pretty cool.
Just like those old movies my grandfather used to watch on some
old machine called a "DVD player." Well, before our neighbors
took it. The quality may have been poor and the films tacky, but
it certainly made me prepared for the coming attack.

 I saved for years and being an inconspicuous child, I
snuck past lines of people while they were still dazed and spent
my life savings on rations. After all eleven dollars were gone, I
had eight candy bars to show for it. Caramellos in fact, because I
remembered in school that liquids and solids are important. Solid
chocolate; liquid caramel. I figured if my grandfather and I were
careful, it would last us a week.

 Eventually we saw the soldiers on the wall screen
marching down the street, and people suddenly felt confidence as
that noble flag bravely did wave. Many silenced their poor
habits, standing tall and free of their panic. Others were put into
a deep fervor, but the tear gas that consumed even the smoke of

the burning cities left them without much but streaming tears of anger. I saw the shaking camera capture the images of soldiers, clad in their protective green, all lined into a perfect formation. They raised their rifles, tanks, and other various armaments. Suddenly I understood why we never had textbooks in school, and why if you lost your pencil, you were out of luck. And when we stared at our crystal quality wall screen with cameras fixated so neatly on the bullets as they soared skyward, I also understood why we didn't much permeate our own atmosphere. Besides, I thought I read somewhere that one of the Hubble descendents found the edge of the universe, and currently, we were almost dead center; so why bother?

The ships pierced our sky and great balls of blue mist poured off the spheres. It was the biggest hail I had ever seen. The fire of our noble soldiers froze before impact and some shells shattered, others, mostly the tank shells, fell to the ground in various regions of the country before they detonated. Soon the spheres slammed into the ground and the ships melted away. Under the cool water were the strangest folks I'd ever witnessed. Blue-skinned and very frail. They were armed with icicles and zero-kelvin guns. Their angry faces quickly turned confused. Landing in the major cities as they did, there wasn't much left to loot and plunder, not to mention surrounding fire. They started to panic and ran all over the place. Many turned gooey liquid straight away; others collapsed and seemed to suffer intense hyperventilation before death.

It made sense, considering they were from the coldest planet known to us. The people ceased their tears and whimpers for mercy and slowly closened to the people of Pluto. They tapped them lightly with their feet and found them to be quite gooey, like an overcooked marshmallow. Everyone kind of looked around and shrugged. Soon everything was back to normal. Our neighbors apologized to my grandfather and returned his ancient DVD player.

It should also be noted that some of those Pluto-folk ended up landing off-course into Nunavut, Canada where the temperature was suitable. They sweat constantly, and often cool off near the artic circle, but I hear they ended up pacifying themselves when they realized the attack was unsuccessful. We couldn't grasp explanation of how cold fusion worked to send them home, so we sent Canada a "thank you" letter for taking them of our hands. Now they are peaceful fishing people with the Inuit tribes. I hear they are expanding their business to Greenland.

It must have been when I was admitted to college when the next invasion trickled through the vine. I heard there were some folks near Alpha Centari who are very sensitive to sound. Heard a beep of some from an early radio device in the late 1800's and got pissed off royally. We ourselves heard from a small unknown newspaper that specialized in the paranormal, founded since the Pluto attack, that those people (?) near Alpha Centari were coming in a major way. Soon the article circulated into bigger places and the government told everyone to calm down, because it was just a hoax, but the dike had split open too far by that point. On a side note, the original reporter died in a freak car accident shortly after publication.

People were in a terrible fuss over the whole thing. First the public started going into a buying frenzy, the man with the economic sense won out, but when supplies grew dim, the strongest fist took over. Luckily, I was still in a small town, so I didn't get involved in most of the rioting. Big cities everywhere were on fire again. And Pluto fish sales were up 300%. Funny how there were still months left until the attack. I sat around waiting, going to my classes and such, and I kept seeing on the wall screen that another oil line had burst when they tried to put the fire out. Then when the supplies were replenished, more news about Alpha Centari broke out of confidential news sources and people rioted again. People must have been awful hungry.

Some of my close friends, who also were lax about the situation, meaning those who stayed on campus, made me a mix album for my music player, and it had a lot of hits of the oldies on it. *We Didn't Start the Fire* by Billy Idol, *Beds are Burning* by Midnight Oil, and *Fire* by Franz Ferdinand. It was pretty funny.

Too bad those lax friends weren't lax enough though. Almost all eventually left, except for my roommate who slept most of his days away. A letter delivery must have fouled up as well, because nobody came to the graveyard to help me bury my grandfather. Not even the preacher. Had to leave me when I needed him most. Thought a lot about those old movies with all the ruckus we used to watch, but I guess it didn't matter much. The actors in those films were probably long dead too. So corny, but so true.

Soon the moment came, and the soldiers passed again and readied themselves. They waited. And they waited. They waited some more. After several weeks they packed up and left. The public was glad traffic decreased. We thought that maybe with the planet's rotation they got China, but we didn't hear any ruckus. In the end it turned out they missed us, which we grew to accept. It is hard enough to navigate a tiny planet with a compass, much less navigate a space vessel through light years. I also think I heard that the same Hubble descendent claimed they accidentally veered into a black hole some solar systems away.

Reports claimed the sheer concentration of radio waves and the like threw off their piloted systems. One might say we are pretty loud for a planet, or as those smarmy Brits would say, "The America of the universe. Bwa bwa bwa." I like to pay my bills online though, it's so convenient. I'm also glad I don't live 300 years in the future, because if one beep pissed off the people near Alpha Centari, well…

So things were a bit quieter in space, and we got back to dealing with other countries on Earth like we were used to. Suddenly the Jupitarians were angry with us, and there I was, wondering if I'd be okay. We heard in the debriefing that communicated and translated services discovered they were angry at our misuse of gas, like we were coming to reap their supply. We could barely make the moon, much less the giant gas ball, but I had a cleanly pressed uniform and engraved dog tags, so it was okay. They must not have even known it was liquid, we just called it gas, and it wasn't like there was much left anyway. The Jupitarians were very sensitive on the matter. That may have been our toughest battle yet, for Jupiter is large and powerful, its sheer gravity alone would make warriors a force to be reckoned with. The prospect of interstellar travel only made their potential technology all the more nerve-rattling.

Their first attack came as routine intimidation, we learned the technique well in boot camp. They had harnessed a fraction of the mighty ever-constant storm that raged the skies. capable of demolishing all structures, though wafer-thin and from gas made. The intense energy flux shorted out most of Earth's electricity for several hours, only those with generators had light. Soon the pulse of the storm passed, and our eyes turned skyward. This tiny fraction, still larger than any earthen storm soared toward us at a very consistent destructive pace. We saw the tiny speck grow in size as it approached. I think I recall a weatherman crying. You should have also seen the grown, war-seasoned men who fell to their knees and wept. Some of them even prayed toward the heavens for any god to spare their children and wives. My bunkmate prayed for his dog to find shelter. A chocolate lab, he loved that mutt. Those of us who remained composed secretly all whispered our own death sentence and hoped for safe passage to the beyond.

But then an odd thing happened. Being a gaseous planet, they must not have had clear line of sight, because coincidentally Phobos, the moon of Mars, obliterated. Then I guess Phobos and the moon must have been in alignment, because the great storm nicked our moon and decimated a portion of it. The tides collapsed from their heights forever more and surfers worldwide were totally bummed. The moon looked really weird afterward, stuck in crescent form. Wiccans were pissed. Crazies didn't really have anything to blame their actions on either.

Anyway, the collisions with the various planetary satellites caused a negative reaction on the storm; the asteroid dust collected most of its energy. Soon the storm hit us even smaller. The storm's energy shifted and melded with our atmosphere, and the storm's physical nature brewed. I had moved to Seattle around two years prior, so this massive storm just made me think that it was raining a little bit less than usual. Granted, the size of the storm on Jupiter was huge before they had broken it up, so naturally this storm, though much weakened, was devastating. It covered the entire nation and it sprinkled for weeks. Flash flooding took many lives before government took action. We had plenty warning for the coming storm, but the nation didn't really create any sort of preparation. Luckily we soldiers were mobile, and we moved operations to a nearby large hill, because a mountain wasn't really necessary with the small flooding we faced.

On the plus side, the fresh water shortage we were gradually facing ended the day the storm struck. And I remember my fellow soldiers showing off pictures of their kids in bathing suits in the constant rainfall. I couldn't believe the dedication of the postal service, but I guess they meant it when they said "sleet, rain, or snow…"

I thought at the time the history books would remember most, assuming they didn't get too soaked in the downpour, the great meteor shower that fell harder than any rain. The myriad moon particles hit like tears. Our forever weeping moon finally held back no longer. The tear droplets crashed earthbound with rupturing force, true sorrow in its now deformed face. Soon the Man on the Moon fell to a lulled sleep, a permanent drooped-eye look graced it. Phobos must have sensed this and too cried, for many of its tears almost punctured our bases and homes. Countries the world over were touched by the sadness, nothing left but an empty crater with salted rubble.

Luckily, a majority of void-ridden tears split into tiny particles that disintegrated in our atmosphere. It was the most beautiful light show I'd ever seen, the entire sky looked of quickly snuffed matches with a delicate purple hue that rippled and turned as the storm fought to maintain itself. Speaking of Ms. Luck, the craters, though pock-marked on our paved-over world of sleek solid surfaces, turned into great lakebeds, and all those flooded cities soon dried out. No desert went thirsty that day.

The storm was an excellent distraction, a cloak perhaps. The clouds barred our vision from that beyond, wrapped in our cool blanket that suspended itself skyward. The lightning too aided this; numerous radar and transmission devices malfunctioned as our electromagnetic fields bent to its whim. Eventually the clouds parted, and many swimming centers went out of business. Mere hundreds of miles from us though, was a greater threat than the death of the local city swimming pool, and that was the vision of strange gas balls dissipatating as they came nearer. At first it looked nothing more than the Aurora Borealis, but we knew when cleverly pointed out the truth of the matter. It was broad daylight, and we were a southbound base.

These giant, dispersed gas clouds revealed solids beneath them, the stench of death peaking out. Civilians that ignored our warnings to evacuate started to flee and loot instinctually. We took aim, and waited for a clear shot. We soldiers almost broke formation, having heard from documentaries dated over one hundreds years ago about wars fought with poisonous gasses. Gasses that leaked into the lungs and through the cracks of the eyes and burned. They dried out the insides nicely until they flaked apart and turned into fresh jerky. This gas was an airy mustard color that started to simmer around us. Our gas masks donned.

The Jupitarians arrived. They didn't appear happy. All had a permanent scowl on their face, loose and sagged, due in part to the constant spa-like effects they lived within. I did note their remarkably clear pores, which were easy to spot even in the fog that amassed us. They were bald with skin that almost shined under the newly birthed sunlight. Their military uniforms looked like a mix between an old-fashioned zoot suit and those foil spacesuits I always saw people wear in the movies my grandfather watched. All of it was a mix of light violet, which actually went remarkably well with their dark orange-splotched flesh. Jupitarian hands held peculiar weapons that smoked and were lumpy, formed from the gas they road in on.

The most intimidating part wasn't their scientific knowledge of air-based chemicals, however, it was their size. Being from a planet of enormous gravity, their bodies fit the concept. Their skin, like the weapons, steamed at a lazy rate, but instead were solid. They giants to us, easily over nine feet tall each. And those were the short Jupitarians. Their strength was equally massive, as we judged by the cracked pavement below their feet. One well placed grapple would grind our bones to dust for daily bread.

Somewhere the first shot heard round the solar system rang, and we followed our fellow brother in suit. Casings scattered everywhere and a thicker, new smoke covered the vanished fog. The order for cease-fire came and we fell back. When the smoke cleared the Jupitarians stood quite annoyed. Surely to withstand such pressure and ravaging storms, their skin too was thick, bulletproof in fact.

They raised their weapons to respond our attacks and took aim true, when a smelly spray blasted us. It frazzled our hair, and were left confused what it meant. The Jupitarians were befuddled too, adjusting their weapons and inspecting them. The Jupitarians with melee weapons cracked a gaseous whip at us. It tickled furiously, like a goat licking one's heels. The whip burst into a small, deformed cloud and faded away. All of the weapons did. The Jupitarians were then in utter shock. I supposed they expected their weapons to hold shape on a planet based around solids.

We commenced our victory claps, but were interrupted as they raised their meaty arms, a gust of wind messed our hair up beyond salon's heal. Our morale wavered. We were armed with cheaply produced Kevlar body armor, with reasonably up to date rifles, and there we were about to be crushed by the meaty paws of a Jupitarian. We banded together and faced our goliaths, for we were an army of one. The leader of the pack lifted his muscular leg and brought it forward. The rest did so in a singular fashion. We swallowed deeply. They had heard of this army-of-one concept too.

Their legs collectively fell, and a miniature earthquake rumbled. Lightning cracked across the concrete. We toppled from our Spartan holding grounds. We guarded our faces with our arms, despite knowing we'd be folded under the impact of brutal blows. Nothing came. No more earthquakes, only guttural moans.

We looked from behind our skin shields and saw the Jupitarians laid upon cracked concrete. They grasped about, some managing to drag themselves away. We didn't really know quite what to think, maybe another clever military strategy, until it dawned on us. Being from a gaseous planet, they weren't used a solid environment. As a result, they likely floated for much of their lives and never learned to walk. So they stayed on the ground, very frustrated, helpless.

A few weeks later, we were given release from our drafted positions, and most of us got back to what we were doing before, which wasn't all that inspired. The government experts on extraterrestrials, a now non-confidential organization that had been around since before the 1950's, organized themselves to collect the Jupitarians from their Earthly prison. "They blocked traffic too much," the reason given when the organization showed up in their plumbing and electric vans with company names never heard prior.

If not for their attempt at killing everyone on Earth, I almost would have felt bad for the Jupitarians. The ones who didn't learn to crawl away flopped their arms in tuckered motions. When the net was thrown to drag them away, their scowled face dragged into sad-puppy-dog origami, and I was reminded of beached manatees.

Some of the Jupitarians dragged themselves to safety, which was evident by trail marks left behind. In small number they didn't hurt anybody, so they were left well enough alone. It also turned out the smoke that emanated from their skin was the correct composition of chemicals needed to fix the hole in the ozone. And several months after they fell from grace, map and Mexican food sales were up, way up. It wasn't the only time I wish I would have invested in stock.

It has been almost two decades since then. Now I am hearing on the old wall screen, an outdated model now, that the Saturnians are coming. Guess they don't want to be the only planet their side of the solar system that hasn't attacked us. Luckily Neptune hasn't word of this, and heaven help us all if the people of Uranus were the violent type.

In any case, the nation requests to donations and recyclables, all plastic materials. Throwing away your empty water bottle means riding with Saturnians. The saying doesn't make much sense, I know, but it inspires well enough. Hula-Hoop production is up 400%, and I wish I would have bought stock when I had the chance. *When does a man learn?*

As I am sitting here reflecting on the beings of space, I realize that we've been through a lot in this past century, and things happen in the now that was speculative crazy talk in the past. I also understand now that only one planet can really keep us down and that's-

Suddenly a large hand busts my door down, and I see the unpleasant orange-splotched skin. Hairless with padded armor, a Jupitarian crawls very slowly across my floor, and knocks over all my good china my grandfather left me. As the thing finally comes toward me with piercing Jupitarian loyalty, I step roughly three feet out of the way. He passes by grumpily and busts through my back door, but not before he knocks all my pans off the countertops. I *was* going to have spaghetti tonight. Damn Jupitarians.

Road Kill

I was shaken awake when the car went over a generous dip. Literally bouncing into consciousness, my irritation started anew. My old pals from college were whooping and hollering about past frat events.

I shouldn't have said old pals, but rather, recently old pals. I had signed the lease for my own studio apartment, away from the condensed dorms that lacked their privacy, and the professors who hounded me for research papers. Before I got the call that wrangled me into a party's attendance that harkened back to somewhat younger days. I was about ready to unpack boxes full of products I ordered off some bargain our-junk-is-your-treasure website. I already had the multi-colored, decorative party lights in the shape of cactuses up, and I almost mounted the fake buck head wearing a sombrero and sunglasses when I got the call. To add to the eventual mistake of agreement, the abrupt phone ring caused me to drop the buck head on my falsely laid footing. Naturally, I rebounded in pain against a table and shattered a bottle of the freshest Tabasco sauce.

I guess I must have looked awful clumsy, but the only one laughing was a bodiless prankster. I was even clumsier with my schedule, when I forgot about my new job. Assembling, checking designs, lifting, taking notes, what a hassle. Trying to increase the decrease of the kind of crease a car gets on collision.

Imagine the higher ups saying in their demanding voices, "Accidents are up! Higher than last decade's. We need safer cars, more stars! I wanna see the night sky when see reviews for this new model. "

In my mind, I rattled off my day because of exhaustion, and a man can't rest when he makes his word to pseudo-brothers. It was in my future taxi I learned who would be sober-cabbie for my drunken escorts. I remembered this old trick. Last guy in is the man without drink. Sometimes found it a little peculiar I got picked up last most of the time, even in those college days.

So I tried getting some shut-eye before I risked falling asleep at the wheel later. My so called friends didn't make it easy though. If not poor driving, I'd be bumped awake by human forces. Some catchy song would always be on the radio too. This particular moment entailed something about bringing sexy back. It had a nice tune, but I didn't understand the lyrics much. Forced awake, I decided to try my hand at staying such a way for the night. As I stretched the vanishing sleep from my body, I slumped against the passenger window.

When I peered out, the radio switched to some discussion by various popular musicians on charity concerts. This was about the dangers of roadway expansion cutting into numerous innocent animals' habitats. They claimed efficient transport cut off valuable food supply and confused critters into taking a steel grill tackle. Then they spoke of orphans and the new problem arising in Singapore, when one of my buddies transmuted desires to donate back to static-laden heavy metal, with but a turn of the dial.

Good riddance, I thought. World problems weren't a concern after a snuff of the Sandman's dust. Besides, more roads meant more reason to drive, with all the more reason to buy a car. Job security. Pleased enough, my head bonked into the window. I saw the red illuminated itself in a mechanical copy of the sunset before us. As the dull thump in my skull subsided, I supposed somewhere during my scattered points of consciousness the highway had transmuted into a small town. Seemed many an alchemist was out tonight. There were small hardware, gas, and coffee-based stores surrounding, but all seemed futile against the trees' servitude waiting ahead. Noble trees stood, making way for our path. What honor bestowed us quelled by way of mysterious speck moving through the forest.

Rubbed my eyes to get this dust particle gone, but it got bigger, and kept growing. Soon this speck, this tiny flicker through the trees, split itself in two and changed forms. The lead speck turned humanoid, and the follower, beast. Almost bursting from woodland, I saw too clearly. It was a man, dressed in neon orange, plaid and a large cap. He struggled desperately with a pine, his footing loose and sloppy, but the thing that followed tore him from the branched arms of safety. Perspiration descended as I watched what horrible sight followed. The man crawled away and shifted his pace, sprinting once on his feet. The beast, with branches atop its head cut the man off and slammed him against the tree. The man, ever so little in the distance, raised up his arms in hopeless attempts to hold the beast's sharp fury.

The beast rose and was shallowly bathed in limelight green. I was rapidly pulled toward the man's nightmarish sight, yet I sat still. I passed by and time seemed to run in single frames, no longer a solid motion. The midnight hooves of this wood demon flailed downward, tearing clothing and flaying flesh. Chunks of meat were shredded into remnants of their past cohesion. What was left of the standing figure, nameless and now faceless, was punctured by the branches of this familiar beast. His body tossed to the side, like a discarded doll, his neon orange jacket reminiscent of a traffic cone. Red mist floated in the air, creating a cover for this beast that placed its maw upon the man's corpse to feed.

From what I saw, I could almost hear the gnashing of bone and the slurps of tenderized flesh. When I grew parallel to the beast, it paused; ears perked and lifted its brutal head. I swear I saw it make malignant eye contact with me, knowing. Despite the cover of trees and subsiding mist, I could see all-too-clearly its piercing eyes, expressionless toward the act it had committed, as though a simple everyday venture. Its snout a moist ruby red, it reacted not to the small droplets of slow oozing liquid that drained itself from the branch-patterns adorning its head.

As the clock, and my heart, resumed their pace I turned, flush-faced, to my comrades. They sang with the radio, jeering some new diva always seen in the headlines at the grocery store. I hadn't even realized it was still on. I guess I must have looked like I just stepped in from the rain, because my buddies chuckled that I had the hots for the slightly off-key woman. Shortly thereafter, the more serious of pals asked if I was okay, looking faintly sick as I was. I asked them all how they could be so damn calm after what just happened. Yet, despite my efforts and reconstruction of events, not a single one witnessed the woodland hunt. They played me off like I was having a nightmare. I guess I was only awake for two or four minutes. It seemed so much longer. Maybe they were right, I was a little groggy. I shrugged it off as a nightmare merged in reality and tried to settle back to sleep. Before I shut my eyes, I saw a raccoon with tire marks tattooed upon it, eternally sleeping as flat as possible. *Heh, road kill*, I thought, and closed my eyes.

Another bump from busted shocks launched me forward, further weakening the integrity of my collar bone. I understood then why it is the most commonly broken bone. I tended the wound and stared out the passenger window again. Everything had a slight glaze to it, which made my world fuzzy. Dreamily I gazed, until my eyes met with a most foul and diabolical creature.

Its head held growing trees, pointed tips that glistened in the direct beam of sunlight peeking over the horizon. They were brown without bark, innocent enough to hang a hat on, but dangerous enough to skewer. How peaceful those expressionless eyes were, a being disguised of pure and noble spirit. Its snout clean and dry as the plains roamed. Even its tan-brown fur was deceptive, slowly giving way to white underneath. Only I knew its dark, sullen nature. Motionless it stood. It waited for the first move. Our standoff was that of the gods, our immortality threatened by even the beat of a heart. I would sit eons if need be, for my fury was just and true. Let my vision slay.

Just then the driver of point A to B leaned in and asked if I was getting out of the car so he could lock the door. Shaken from my heightened throne I fell into reality. I guess I must have looked like the challenged friend brought out of pity, staring with my furrowed brow as I did.

Around this beast were other people like me. Clothes, two legs, human, they had it all. Not to mention convenient disposable plastic cups likely filled with some brand of ale or lager. I crept from my taxi and felt solid tar under foot. The thing stood like some piñata, mocked, beaten and leaned against by many, compared to its real life counterpart. A fake. Quite a realistic fake, but a fake nonetheless.

It appeared to be a deer, more specifically a buck, made of ceramic. I think it was ceramic; I was no expert on lawn decoration. Probably plaster. There was a similar animal, sans antlers, that seemed to lay subservient nearby. I guess I must have seemed pretty foolish when I worried my pals like I did. Up close this decorative animal truly was peaceful and kind. It appeared less powerful and foreboding, and all I wanted at that point was to scratch its ears. My worries sloughed off sore, tired bodybuilder's shoulders and returned anew to my regular, refreshed shoulders. Though I did have a kink in my neck from sleeping oddly.

When darkness swallowed us whole we denied the moon's dull stage-lit embrace. Inside I found myself wrapped in discussion of little relevance. Almost everyone talked to Sir Alcohol, and were too wrapped up in his clever folly to make much effort elsewhere.

I had remembered learning one day in college that Dionysius, god of drink, was also the inspiration behind theatre. And so it appeared despite their separation, drama and drink would eventually always join hands. I avoided this, however, when I dragged my friends toward my taxi. Confiscating keys, I rang out a call to my allies for their free fare. They eased to this suggestion by way of foul-felt bellies and dizzied perceptions. The normally transparent marionette strings upon them grew material the more they took lip to drink, so difficult to corral they were not.

In my attempts, one friend slumped into me, which pushed me off stable foot into a sharp object. Prodding carefully, I found the object to be the lawn ornament I confronted earlier. I guess I must have looked pretty girly when I yelped, because my inebriated jerks were laughing at me. As I directed them to the car, my wince was the congratulation to empty fears, a small scratch from my collision marked the occasion.

Confident in my wrangling, I tossed my ten-gallon hat as an adieu to the party that excited about as easily as standard investment meetings. I dusted my old hat off and placed it tenderly upon mine head, clicking the meter of favors due.

The drive from point B to A was worse than vice versa. Perhaps because I sat as the driver, my buddies were even more raucous than usual. But it didn't feel right either. Every moment behind the wheel seemed more hesitant, cautious. I decided to take the longer, yet brighter, louder path home. Sorry Frost, can't risk the road less traveled this time.

Perhaps the distraction kept my mind silent, like going to a carnival trying to comprehend clowns. Even though far from home, we ended up finding the way back after getting past the branching curves of the neighborhood. Ready to turn the wheel, something blocked our path.

I turned the brights on and what stood before the reckoning of a car was a shoddily-built sign. It was hard to make out with all the dirt and grime, but I thought it read "detour," what with the arrows it had. I was surprised at the condition this city kept their signs in. Its reflective color now dull and sullied, I would have driven straight into it, if not for the red octagon that slowed me. Additionally, some bolts appeared to be missing from the bottom bar of thin metal, and partially collapsed on the street. Those folks involved in road construction must not have taken care of their equipment, but that's when I thought it. I was almost certain I had heard on the news that they started construction on the road after they finished that new highway, but

that was months ago. I figured the people involved were paid
hourly, and thus lazy about the entire thing.

Not wanting to risk the fine involved, I turned the wheel
in guided arrow's direction. When the car shifted to a new street,
I could see the houses thinned themselves out in the distance.
Something caught my eye then. Maybe the reflection of the
headlights incandescence, but it captured my attention fully.

My nervousness felt justified when I witnessed the beast.
Its eyes red and piercing, I was hypnotized to its gaze. I broke
suddenly, much to my companions' complaints, and tried to
verify my vision. I peered with appraiser's eyes, contemplating
return to the party to slumber until the morrow. My friends
disagreed, one of them complaining they'd missed too many days
work already, hung over or not.

After careful thought, I considered it another coincidence.
After all, that house looked similar to the party's, which looked
like all the other houses in the area, very townhouse. Even the
hanging plants seemed the same. No doubt they had the same
regulatory lawn decoration. Satisfied with my own conclusions, I
decided instead of testing my theory I would tear through the
road to home. As I pealed out, the ornamental beast seemed to
follow me with its eyes. I didn't desire direct eye contact, but
could have sworn its head turned, following, in the corner of my
eye.

I reached the straight shot home. The highway I'd taken
up. If I drowned myself in the wanton needs of my friends'
requests to fill their cavernous gullets, I could remain distracted
from the trees harrowing influence upon me. I took in all the
conversation, the radio, and swam, my body on cruise control.
The latest song was about someone not wanting someone else's
boyfriend. This made sense to me, if they were really friends, or
the boyfriend was a jerk. The segmented lines on the road came
and went, came and went.

They led my vision deceptively from hypnotic
mindlessness to a detective's trail. The clues were there, the
footsteps and discarded possession that glittered under headlights.

There it lay, beaten and scarred, resting with dying breath against a tree. The force of impact wrapped the metallic carriage, in an unwilling hug, about the tree. The carnage exposed its hastened embrace, its hood popped, doors nearly discarded in the same way as glass once held. I saw no passenger, nor sign of presence, as though the vehicle took itself for a joy ride.

I wanted to stop, to investigate. What if the driver was long gone? What if he passed away in some ditch for carrion crows delight? What if he made it to aid? What good would salvage on a moonlit night bring? Better to keep on and hope, hope the man's own folly through likened drunk ordeal led him to that situation.

My friends found it "cool" and desired to stop and observe the wreck. I berated them with discarded tones, and kept on. My eyes concentrated fully on the speedometer; never seemed to get high or fast enough to escape the cowardice in my mind. My hands were too moist from sweat to grip the wheel as tight as I should have, and the air conditioning wouldn't get any colder. I swore I'd buy my friend a bottle of that AC-chill when we reached home.

In my intense, hunched demeanor I became most vulnerable, for jester friends had gotten into a childish, yet playful, scrap. One fist wavered, lost its aim and struck a most valuable commodity, the driver.

At that point I wish that specific friend would have listened to me when I said gym memberships were a waste of money. My clammy hands slipped off the steering wheel. In my attempts to readjust, I had swerved over one lane, back to the other, and onto the shoulder. I had almost collided with dense woodland, but determination brought us back at the nick. I turned toward my friend steadfast with steel convictions. Being drunk, he shrugged it off as no great ordeal. After I managed to turn my stiff neck back, I saw the thing in the road that knocked me out.

I woke up with my head resting against the steering wheel. My stay came with a complimentary splitting headache. I stayed there a while, thinking. I hadn't seen clearly what I hit, but it looked like it was made of ceramic, or maybe plaster. I wasn't sure. Maybe neither. I guess I must have looked pretty hot-headed to my friends when I shouted my way into a crash. I eventually got the gumption to lift my head, but it was much stiffer than a few seconds ago. Everything was fuzzy at first, and my vision repelled itself from harsh moonlight reflected from the dash. When the war drums in my head slowed their beat I was given mercy. This mercy gave to mind only, for my eyes were cursed with a terrible sight.

I sat motionless; luckily my foot had fallen off the accelerator in the crash, but something under the hood smoked. Not too good for its health I figured, but who was I to stop it? It looked a mighty fine dent from my viewpoint too. That wasn't the worst part. I surveyed the car to see how my friends managed. One of my pals in the backseat moaned some sort of wicked death cry. He was vomiting and shaking all over. Didn't even look up when I tried to snap him out of it. Just kept his head against my seat and shook. Never a colder man there was, even his skin turned from vibrant peach to subtle gray.

Another friend was gone, and that's what shocked me more. After the accident, he must have been so disoriented that he fled the car to escape the mess, seek help. And yet I felt something more. The car door was open and a brisk breeze blew in, cool and dry. Out there, the woods. I didn't know if I should have sought him out, followed, dragged him back to the car, to the hospital. I didn't even know how much time had passed, as the clock-radio seemed to be off.

My friend next to me, sitting passenger seat, looked worst off. His seatbelt wasn't tightened properly, and the tug of collision almost tore the belt completely through. He was just laying there. Plip-plips kept coming from him, that strawberry syrup falling slowly, clinging gooey, and oozing from his ruby-yet-purple lips. It settled finally in a small pool by his shoes he bought two weeks ago. It seemed that strawberry syrup easily complimented the pancake he possessed, with rum butter sauce inside. The glove box dash was not kind in giving way. His head like a deflated balloon. I didn't check to see if he was only sleeping it off.

The key in the ignition turned to no avail. Seemed the battery was dead. Or possibly something else loosened on impact. The hood seemed crimped shut in the accident anyway, so there wasn't a thing to do.

My thoughts brought forth no satisfactory option to pursue. The smell of blood in the car made my stomach churn, and already I felt poorly from lax reaction to my close friends' injuries. I rubbed my temples to scare away the monks, but their drummers beat their barrels harder, driving me to action.

The car was dead as two of my passengers, but I wasn't going to let my last hope at personal salvation perish on me. It was like that movie, with those guys in the Air Force. *Never leave your wingman.* Together we stand, separated we fall. All that emotional junk. Then I remembered the most important fact of all; I had made a promise. And a man seldom rests when a promise is made to his pseudo-brothers. That promise was to watch out for my drunken buddies. I tried my best, but I wasn't finished.

Shoving my shoulder to the door, it cracked open and I fell to the road. So it became that my little drummer boys grew into strong men with hammers, *parumppapapum*. I tried to stand, but ended up falling against the door. The second attempt was successful, using the hood for leverage. I staggered in front of the car and felt something wet and slimy beneath my feet. Supposed it must have rained while I rested, or some such thing. Needless to say, there was nothing lying in front of the car. I readied and pushed off the car, walking steadily toward the forest.

My great efforts were rewarded with a quick rest against pine. My heavy breathing seemed to be in tandem with another sound nearby. I was surprised I hadn't heard it before, as it sounded quite like a distinct wheeze or shuffle sound. I gripped the tough bark and forced myself forward, my eyes dull and heavy. No wonder my shock was stilled. All I felt was sleepy dust quietly sprinkled. All the trees looked the same, and I barely made the car out from my vantage point. The sound was closer, more distinct. It sounded like wind pushing aside tree branches with whistled moans. There were also sounds of rolling dried leaves and burbling brooks.

Small saplings were suddenly decorated with plaid parchment, denim, and even a shoe. The ground held more junk; nylon, small pieces of scattered metal, smashed radios and a lantern. I'm sure to some this would have looked like Christmas, all this trash someone else's treasure, but it wasn't the right season. No snow laid there to compliment it all. I slowed my steps and walked cautiously. I peered between branches to see where the normally peaceful sounds of nature came from. I could make out a faint glow in the small opening. The culprit must have been another discarded lantern, or possibly flashlight, its batteries exhausted and dimming out.

The sights I witnessed were no scene one would find hanging in the usual restaurant chains, painted by some mass-produce artist. My entire perception of sound turned out terribly askew. It was that beast again, the rest of his kind banded together. Few held a crown of branches atop their heads, but they were one in the same.

Only one stood out in particular, larger than the rest. He appeared bathed in blood, perhaps out of glorified ritual for a leader. Its large horns had grown so tall and with such girth, I was surprised the beast wasn't rooted to the ground. Supposed nature had granted movement to a defected beast, for despite the powerful presence of the horns, portions were cracked, broken off. And the expressionless eyes were incomplete, for one was bulbous and sealed, as though swelled shut. He lowered his head deeper as a moist munch spurted from its maw.

They fed most aggressively, and it was only when they pulled their heads up to swallow morsels did I see the detail necessary to imprint my mind. Some stranger lay there, clothes unbuttoned or, more likely, torn. His rib cage lay exposed, like a washed xylophone, some evidence of cracking apparent. Worse yet, specific ribs still gripped precious meat tied in strings, holding the structure together in almost entirety. A face untouched, frozen and agape. Never deeper were the wrinkles for his age. Perhaps it the leg with bones jutting disturbed most of all. Symbolic of the escape he attempted. But like the man seen in my previous arrested gaze, these attempts remained unsuccessful to the grace of such captors.

The sound of dried leaves was explained through digging hooves into a shell, trying to crack more from this nut who abandoned the safety of metal encasements. This man brought forth no explanation to the rest of the sounds. That title belonged to dear friend of mine. Adjacent, he was collapsed. I never was quite sure, but he seemed alive through this torture, fingers twitching, and fabric moving; though this may have just been the struggled attempts of hungry beasts freeing their feast of its physical form.

A severely split face deformed my friend's appearance. His jaw was shattered and from the crevasse emanated a slight whistle sound, like an intense moan that shrieked as a banshee for the reaper's touch. This moan was off-set, however, with the gurgling of foul-smelling liquids splattering from hoarse coughs. Every hooven press only strengthened the volume of my past friend's cries for mercy.

My hands involuntary pulled the pine's branches apart further, trying to look away, but only being drawn in more. Unfortunately, shocked movement caused something heavy to fall from the tree onto my head, which bounced onto my false-footing. Naturally, I rebounded in pain and slipped onto the ground, piercing my backend with shards of broken glass. A yelp escaped my lip's barrier.

Through the gap in branches I saw the beasts react. They paused and listened intently. I too paused, as their mocked forms had done earlier that night. Soon they parted. The leader limped away, precious liquid sustenance dripped from his underside ground-ward, until it had retreated back into the heart of the forest. A wall of fear blocked my entrance to the sacrificial site. Instead my own physical pain forced me to flee toward the car. I heard it then.

My own footsteps seemed to be doubled behind me, quickened, smarter. I guess I must have seemed like easy prey, because of the forest's disorientation. The repeated blows to my head also made it hard to see. I had become nigh-delirious. I could sense, sense the stab of the blood-red eyes that trailed me. There was no deprivation of intensity. My own flight only warmed their meal, cooking itself thoroughly like a good victim. Perhaps they'd stop by a nearby creek to cleanse their palette afterward. I was scratched on all sides by low hanging branches, and even the concern of poison ivy entered my mind, if I lived long enough to enjoy such an unforgiving itch.

Still I did not slow, finding new twists and turns that led me no nearer to the car than before. What did it matter? Surely such strong beasts could shatter a window in but a moment's time. It would only serve to tire them, making my death all the slower. And surely there was little doubt to their intellectual merits. Perhaps it was they who dragged my friend from the car, instead upon his own capacity. Perhaps this night was planned all too perfectly, with traps and clever ambushes. Eventually my body took no more. My legs burned intense fire, my vision almost vacant, and an altogether sense of helplessness sprinkled as did the needles of a pine.

I slid on dried needles and crouched against a tree. I didn't even have the strength to bother climbing it. I guess I must have seemed awful foolish, relinquishing myself as I did. I even started to unbutton my over-shirt to make it all the more accessible. I waited with bated breath, but was befuddled when no beast bastard bumped me. Every direction vacant, only the wind my companion. And what good friends we were, as neither expected anything of the other. A mischievous companion, however, echoing my footsteps as it had, making me believe the concerts of pursuit. I contained my victorious laugh and leaned too greatly my head against the pine. With a thud the tremors in my mind returned, and a great new maestro took his conducting tool back to percussion, where gnarled gongs produced grated tunes. I squeezed my head and bent forward.

Time passed without meaning, and hot air replaced cool. I reformed my posture and let woodland back into my eyes, but it wasn't woodland that greeted me. A majestic and strong figure stood, its four legs supporting a tree most deceased. The odor of rotting meat flowed from the beast's snout. It had eyes or eye rather. The other a protruding medallion embedded within a malicious skull. I did not waver, nor did the beast, despite its grievous cuts and missing patches of fur. Spittle with flesh bits lightly covered my face against its intimidation-laced snort. The flakes that slid and fell from my face said it all. I guess I must have been awful dumb to have sat there all that time.

Perfectly still, my perspiration flowed vividly from my being onto the gentle pine needles that lay out a bed for my eternal rest. It was a gentle rain that softened said bed and even the moon shrieked a death wail in tribute to me. It was only then that I could hear the larks... Ah to heck with it, I was scared, really scared. All I could think of doing was running. And so I did.

I left from my spot and sprinted. I bumped a tree on my first attempt, but managed to find a clear path in my tunnel vision. I was on the human autobahn, even Jesse Owens would have been deeply envious of how quick my actions were. I thought I had seen a flicker through the trees and the crunch of twigs, maybe even a brush of wind, but it couldn't have caught me that quickly. I was a newfound track star. But this star shined a little too bright in the darkness and I froze.

I knew the area, the sacrificial site. I was led there deliberately. I knew I should have kept moving, but couldn't. A bright light had come from the darkness and held me motionless. A shadow flew through the overwhelming light and into my stomach. It pierced hard against my tightened, yet worn, muscles. The pain stabbed like several syringes; the serum granted me flight.

I wished I could have altered my course and shot upwards into the stratosphere, bursting into a flare signalling help, to slay these foul beasts and avenge our troupe. But when all ended, I knew rescuers would chalk it up to drunken rage, probably satanically-influenced, and leave it at that. No docile disguises decidedly deduced as dangerous.

I sprung against the tough soil and halted against sponge-like material. This sponge soaked me through with sticky water, and immediately chilled my spine. I was practically blanketing the mutilated body of my friend, and that sponge of past more likely an opened intestine tract; he seemed to have eaten vodka-laced watermelon that night. What a repulsive combination.

A beast snorted and tried its hypnotic gaze once more, but I had none of it. I bolted, vowing the traits of the true smartest animal, man. I faltered under the wincing pain of my stomach, holding the coiled rope inside. Almost doubled over, but kept on. That only led to my latest false-footed exploit. My foot caught hold of the hollow cavity in my friend's skull. I slipped on the scattered fragments of said friend's soiled, discarded jaw.

As red ooze splattered upward, I hoped the mist shrouded me enough to escape in my pathetic half-crawling-run. Spiders were better skilled skitterers than any man, for good reason. I was skewered almost instantaneously, shish-kabob. Rapid undead plant life grew from the toreador's cape.

My body proved too marinated in its own juices. Slipping from the branches, I slammed into the nearby pine. Various fresh, baby needles fell on me. The concussion I probably had about did me in. *Luckily,* the sensation of my guts excruciatingly racked to rending, their seams tearing from each other and slowly mixing to new elements, kept me awake for the rest. This was made all the worse when I realized two of my teeth cracked, because I had trouble swallowing a dislodged filling with the viscous blood and bile simmering in my stomach slow cooker. And I just had those fillings done after I got my dental insurance last month.

I feebly attempted to clamber away, but one of my shoulders made a *thwop-pop* against the tree. It didn't end up working too well. The beast drove me through once more and raised my fallen body skyward. At least I could actually see the moon outside the city lights, and it was a nice night too, so cloudless with a moon so full. I thought I saw Mars, until I hit the pine again. I wasn't able to breathe anymore. My ribs hugged too tight and my neck snapped.

It was such a strange sensation that quickly fled with the rest of my senses. Usually you went through life thinking you had your head on straight the whole time, until something unexpected slams into you and makes you pine for something else. Okay, I'm sorry that didn't make much sense, but my headache was worse than ever, the 100-man-band at their final crescendo, and I was so tired of the same tired tune you probably heard on some radio station covered by some new diva.

The beast bit deeply into my hamstrings and dragged me back to the center of the sacrificial site. Once, he lost hold and about tore my leg off, but it didn't hurt anymore. I saw the other beasts like him show up and stare me down. All those red lights stopped it all. Running never did any good, because they caught up to all of us in the end. Anyway, I guess I must have looked awful silly with my head twisted like that, hanging off my body.

The Immortality Process

The box stares at me and I stare back. It is sitting there, affixing my gaze with its sharp, tightly bound, bark-brown paper. I am also sitting; my legs rest firmly on the ground, my arms supporting a sullen head as I look on with concentration. I am wondering what I should do. This peculiar box is very grumpy with me, its neat folds forming a menacing, furrowing brow. We have only just met, and yet, at the same time, I feel I know why it is here. I am going to test my thoughts. I go into the kitchen and rummage about. A bit hard to see here, I have to remember to change that light bulb when I get the chance. Ah, found it. I bring the hammer back to my room and lift it lightly. Not too furious a motion, just giving it a good whack. The hammer strikes and a blacksmith nature consumes me. That is alright, place a few more taps here and there. Now the box is in right ruin, broken and torn.

I place the hammer next to the box. You might wonder why I keep a hammer in my kitchen, but you would understand if you could see the size of this place. Got to keep what you can where you can. I spin around and sit on my bed again; my shoulders slump and I shut down my eyes. Squeeze them so tight I see the dots that swirl, making home on the surface. I make the dots what I am going to see. A box in complete wreckage. One with torn flaps, with no shape similar to the previous square it was. Imploding on itself, tightly-bound paper now loose with sad eyes. Furrowing brows giving way to a depressing realization of fading from pristine glory to junk. Yes, that is what I will see.

I open my eyes with a heavy sigh. Just as I figure, utterly perfect. The box is back in its usual shape, an untouchable cube, the brown paper tight as ever, not even an oily fingerprint can find its home on such a thing. The hammer next to it, also like I figure. It was the same with the matchbook.

Oh yes, I tried to burn the thing, but no luck. It was a singed, charred, and altogether heap of ash. As soon as I blinked, it was whole again.

I scratch my head and meander back and forth in my mind. Parting my thinning hair with my nervously-bitten fingernails must give enough fresh air to the old brain, because it is bringing me back.

I was depressed again. Maybe it was the foul moonlight that struck my studio apartment with a cold pale-blue, as it illuminated all failures in the dark. Maybe it was when I stuck my tongue too far into the deep neck of the voluptuous, and always sultry, bottle of the freshest, bought-from-a-discount-liquor-store, raspberry Schnapps.

Drank a lot of it that night okay? What? It tastes exactly like real fruit! Look, I am trying to tell you my problem here. You any better? Well anyway, I started looking back on my life and all the things I could have changed. Truly I was panged by the past.

I remembered in vivid detail those shortcomings, how my wife had left me and taken the boys to some other state. Said it would help them grow, broaden their horizons. I did not see much of the boys after that. Glad the wife left, she was a broad, but my little guys' laughing obnoxiously at my lame jokes seemed to make the day all worthwhile. Sure, I could have shipped them over during the holidays, but they did not need me anymore. They probably had a stepfather at that point. Heck, even if they did come over, they would only have cereal and basic cable. Kids are bored by such adult ways.

Always so wrapped up in my work, constant overtime. Needed the money I figured at the time. Thought I was making a difference by having two wives, my real one and the job, but it did not end up turning out so well. Eventually got laid off once the big guys changed around. Some merger I heard. Ridiculous. And so there I was, wallowing away in self-pity with only drink to hold my hand through tough times.

Now I am carefully living off my savings and my melancholy thought brings me to a muck-ridden swamp of deep desires. A place where the treasures are vast, but you have to dig deep and dirty to get them. My arms reeked of the metaphorical muck. I staggered to and stained the clear window with my muck-turned-sweat covered arms. A green fever enveloped me, and the sickness followed.

I needed to be great for my kids, to be remembered, as a hero or legend. Something that would make them proud enough to tell their grandkids. And those grandkids would be all shocked and say, "No way," or "nuh-uh," like all precocious children do when their perceptions of reality are challenged. Maybe if disease was cured or people's lives were made more convenient or a book was written that would make people take a moment from their lives to think. Think about all the small things and the fragile frailty of life.

And it is because of those thoughts I got this box. The green disease is contagious, and it gets worse when left festering. But is that not like all fear-worthy diseases? Oh you damn box!

I slurred to the swaying trees through the muffler of glass that I would give anything to live a little longer, until I accomplished something truly memorable. Only a few more years, no, immortality until the feat's finish. The trees talked amongst themselves, but I could not hear their whisper. They must have given mercy, taking pity upon me, because they started to drop their leaves as wind left the party. I thought then that they must have lent me portions each of their own dull, lengthy lives. All of this was to support my cause so that they, immobile, shall too be remembered.

In drunken mind I decided to dedicate a holiday to trees and shrubbery after all was said and done. I thought I remembered one already, but I was real smashed. I started swaying after my holiday to match the movements of the trees' branches. Would be lonely to be immortal, but honorable to be a great dad once more. I fell backwards onto my bed and passed out.

I woke up with my back like thin, splintered plywood bent too far. My head pounded, nails drove into my wooden body. Confused as to when I became part of the lumber-yard, it turned out to be my apartment door trying to free itself of hinges. Probably wanted out when its parents started to sacrifice themselves for my temple of dreams.

I was a little disoriented because my world view was upside-down, which only helped my back you see. I slowly stumbled to the door and tried my best to free it, so the rattling would stop and leave my head be, when I noticed a curious man stood before me. Oh, knocking, of course. A bright smiling man spoke in quick segmented passages.

"Gotta package fer you sir."

Appeared he still had time to be polite. Also had a stale, rigid handsomeness to him. I felt out of place just looking at his fresh, new-on-the-job face. He maintained a courteous smile the whole time and his outfit was crisp and clean. I would have sworn then that he just ironed it, because the man was far too clean-cut for a delivery man, and he emanated heat. I wanted to think it strange for a delivery man to bring the package up this many floors, especially in a secure apartment complex, but I was first-most entranced by his appearance.

He wore a loose, yet professional uniform that matched the box held under his arm. It was probably loose-fitting because of the constant movement through warm weather he struggled with, but a drop of sweat did not make home on his forehead. Pristine and presentable, just like the box that seemed freshly wrapped and handled with nimble worker's care. Trust me, if you had seen this box after a rough night, you too would have thought it was packaged by the king of dry-cleaners and wrapped in clouds as it rode upon shocks that made a car feel like it was flying.

He grew impatient with me as I stared intently on, trying to keep him focused together after the abrupt awakening.

"Say ah gotta package here sir," he said as he dug a board into my chest. "Min' singin' here?" A pen attached to the board along with an omnibus sheet full of big words and microscopic text. I grabbed the board absent-mindedly and stumbled over as I scribbled my name.

"Seems ya had rough night sir."

"Hmm? Oh yes, I suppose I kind of did."

"Hope ya didn' do anythin' 'gretful. Worse kin'," He said as he shoved the box into my arms, forcefully exhaling my lungs. Before I knew what happened, he had already started a brisk pace down the hallway.

"Hey what about these papers!?"

"No worry sir, gotta cover," He waved the board in the air. Never did he stop to turn around. Never noticed he had taken the thing from me. He was quick as a cobra in poked rigor mortis. That makes me seem more cultured does it not? Using Latin?

There, now you are caught up on the recent events, and the box still sits in my gloomy apartment. I would not dare to try opening it the proper way. It probably would not let me either, judging by its rounds with the matches and hammer. The box came with a letter attached underneath from a Mr. Derek Eville. A clever man, that Devil. Takes advantage of you when you least expect it. The letter told me the secret to immortality is inside, but it is not yet ready for the likes of me to open.

I am stuck with this stupid box, after my deal made half-thought, and I do not know what is to be given. A soul is not a profitable stake for a man who cannot die. To succeed but continue on with mortals dropping like victims of the consumption. I am not ready for such a double-edged gift. What a funny thought, *return to sender, location Hell*. Imagine the shipping charges. But you can already guess the fee for such a thing. One day I will bring the box back personally. The late charges will be horrendous. A literal arm and leg. Well, a sober mind might as well continue testing.

The letter told me to bring the box to the local mall on the 14th of August, at a specific moment on the primary Greenwich time zone. A bit of math for my location told me I had until around 4 P.M. I completely understand the Devil does not go by Earth time in his daily life, but have some consideration. Anyway, That is today, but I still have six hours to figure this thing out, get it out of my life. It may regenerate despite the damage, but maybe I can remove the thing from my possession, pawn it off on someone else. Better head to the bus stop.

I feel secure on the bus with all the people on board. They look pleasant enough. A Blind Man with his dog, a nice golden Labrador that still looks youthful and agile. The usual Old Bag Lady with her groceries. Even the generic rambunctious teens flirting with their sole female compatriot. Weakly populated, but safe enough.

I try to greet the golden Labrador, I love dogs you see, but it growls and barks at me. The Blind Man holds him back quick as a lively mongoose. Oh great, worse than I thought. Well, not worse than I thought, I mean, a package from the Devil is about as bad as it comes, but you know what I mean.

I sit juxtapose the Old Bag Lady, and listen to distinct squeals from the girl and giddy laughter from the guys. The annoyance of it all makes it hard to think. Looking up at the Old Bag Lady, she smiles kindly.

"Hullo," the Old Bag Lady says with a noticeable accent. Sounds more Old England than New England.

"Oh, hi," I say back, and return to facing the window. Where can I rid myself of this box? Cast it into the ocean? No, not enough time. Takes at least three or four hours, and that is without traffic. With the "Sellebration" going on in the town nearby, inside the local mall, the roads will be smothered.

Where? Where!? My eyes gaze back to the smiling Old Bag Lady. Hmm… She *is* old, and I am sure she would like to have a little extra time. Make peace. Yeah, I have at least twenty years on her, maybe more. Who would pass on this at such an age? I lick my lips with worrisome anticipation and shuffle my legs for the salesman's phrase to start.

"Lovely day is it not?" Nice start, nice start.

"Oh yes, certainly."

"So… Went grocery shopping?"

"You have the sharp eye don't you?" She said with light-hearted sarcasm.

"Ah yes, I suppose that *is* obvious. I suppose I should have said, 'You going to eat all of that yourself'?"

"No, no, course not. Doctor is always on me about me cholesterol. Why, if I ate what is in this bag, he'd kill me himself." There was obvious contempt for her physician, because her lip quivered slightly, as though she would instantly fill the bus with saliva from years of unsought cravings. "These are ingredients for a birthday cake. Three layers high!"

"Birthday eh? For whom?"

"My little Daryl, he's a right nice chap. Just on my way to pick up his present in fact. On the way home it is."

"Not taking advantage of the 'Sellebration'?" I inquire.

"No no, don't like the big crowds. Have this big bad feeling about the whole situation. Wouldn't go there today."

"Yeah, I know what you mean. *All too well.*" This was it! All of it gold! A package, a birthday, a lady in need of a package for a birthday. "You know, if you want to save the trip and the crowd, I have this package I was looking to return, but you can have it if you want. I am sure anybody would want something like this. It is *very*, very special indeed."

"And why give it to me? What is it?"

"Glad you asked. Um… It is the newest game, *Warhawks: This Time I'm a Falcon.* The newest game everyone wants. It is all the rage."

"I don't think Daryl would like that. Sounds awful violent."

Should have made up something prettier.

"Where did you get a game everyone wants anyway?"

"Uhm… Games Lot? It was on sale?"

"Isn't Games Lot back thataway?" She questioned, pointing behind her.

Darn! I did not realize it is a real place. Right in the mall too. Back thataway. Bad call. I think of the only thing I can do. I extend the box, "What if I told you this box could make you immortal?"

"Shove off. I don't take packages from strangers. Not from ruffians."

"Ruffia-look lady, *please*, I am begging you now. How much do you want to-" Suddenly I cut off. I pause for a moment with my wallet split open and see two boys staring back at me from the tiny plastic jackets inside. Their rosy cheeks with smiles somewhat toothless seem to represent the cracks, the holes, in my lame attempts. Their little T-ball uniforms remind me of the games I used to watch.

A bunch of clueless sprouts running around trying to catch a ball, even the kids up to the plate. Surely every parent there felt that warmth in their hearts, and maybe this Old Bag Lady herself had kids, maybe she did not. Maybe "little Daryl" was a pet name for her husband, maybe not. I could feel their warm cherubic cheeks turning from a flowing red to a shameful one. Awful a thing to pawn it off on this Old Bag Lady.

Even those noisy teenagers became more hopeful. They have their whole lives ahead of them, and I am almost certain my own boys are around the same age by now. Maybe they are cavorting around with some dame like this group. Imagine, my little boys now horn dogs. Makes me chuckle a little. How they used to hate girls. I put my wallet away and apologize sincerely to the Old Bag Lady.

I have become a ruckus because the Blind Man's dog is snapping and snarling, drool furiously pouring from its mouth with bushy fur spiking porcupinewise. The Old Bag Lady is very hostile with her pursing lips and manifold wrinkly forehead. The bus pulls over and my request to leave is met.

I step on the ground and a small cloud of dust bursts onto my feet, soiling them. This is the shadier part of town, with the run down apartments not so many miles from my own. A little risky walking down here alone, but the sun is skyward, shining its crime-deterring beam around me. I do, however, pray that somebody robs me, anybody, I do not care. I look around carefully and meander down an alley. There the light becomes shadow, vacationing darkness whiling away the hours. My shoes crunch already broken glass and I kick an empty can down the dead-end path. Rusty pipes drip water down this shady trail, the air heavy and stale. It smells, albeit faintly, like sulfur.

Approaching a large, smudged green dumpster I stand for a moment to listen. I hear only those drops of rusty water on cracking pavement. In one swift motion I lift the lid of the dumpster and toss the box in. Foul smells force their way into my nostrils and I recoil trying to cover my face. vast numbers of flies zoom out of captivity in the smallest crack as the lid closes.

Back down the alley the smell lingers in the inner reaches of my nostrils, but it feels as though flame anew with the increasing odor of sulfur. Fearing what this means, I am going to run. I think you can pretty much piece it all together. Now that I am running down the streets, I must give off the appearance of a fleeing criminal. I have broken some law with somebody. That much is certain. I look behind and see nothing but myriad flies assailing trash cans producing the same stench. It is interesting because the streets seem so empty. The people are probably inside because of the heat. Maybe they are at the "Sellebration." My heart figures another cause above all those. Less rational, but lingering there in buzzing specks.

Under a little stress right now, so I am going to pause, collect myself, and have a drink to calm my nerves. A little flask full of raspberry Schnapps always does the trick. Okay, so I drink more than every once and a while, and maybe that contributed to my spiraling marriage, but a man has got to work does he not? And maybe he wants to wind down at the end of the day is all. Listen, who are you to judge me? Need to calm my nerves for God's sake. Besides, it has fruit, raspberries, *hello*.

I screw that shining silver cap off and let the warm, yet smooth taste of puckering raspberries slide down my throat. I bring back the flask and screw the cap back on, slipping it back into my side pocket with my wallet, like always. Where there is liquor there is money, they say. Not much, but it helps the nerves. Breathe deep and relax, come on, everyone now. There, I am rid of the plague.

I walk a confident stride down the decaying streets I would call a slum, but it would be an understatement. Cannot be too great for family raising. Shops are up ahead, that must be where the people are. When I begin walking by a trash can on the corner of 9th and Brimstone I think I see something. I begin speed-walking because it is not possible the thing beat me here. You see, the box is sitting on a stack of empty kicked cans and candy wrappers right behind me, but I am not going to pay any heed, let city hall deal with it.

I quickly turn the corner too, because I see a strange truck on the side of the road with some delivery service's name. Lowering my head inconspicuously, the brisk walking gives me away. Every now and then I swear I see the same guy in loose-fitting brown clothes. Cannot really make the person out, but I am sure of it. This sucks. The Devil found me already. I sprint down the sidewalk; placements of my footing surely broke the backs of a hundred mothers, but I did not have time to care. Okay, hundred-seventeen if you are the type to keep count.

Reaching for the handle belonging to a small flower shop, which I too will admit is a smidgen odd for a run down part of the city, I pull lightly and the doors swing open harshly before me, narrowly avoiding their swivel. With sharp sounds, a loud crack shouts as the door busts mostly off its hinges, resting with a *chunk* into concrete. I notice the pleasing chill of any quality flower shop and the pleasant scents it holds and wonder why all doors suddenly seek to escape their entrapments. Changing their ways, letting whole new realms of reality slip outside their holdings.

This particular pocket shows me its true form now, all the flowers wilting and dying away. That foul smell of rotting garbage is back, and… Do I smell raspberries? The lights spark out and a man in loose-fitting brown steps right into my face from the darkness before recognition. A wave of heat washes over my face so fast it burns, like moths coming too close to an innocent looking flame.

"Drop ya box sir," The Devil says to me. Express delivery straight from Hell's bowels. Sinful laxatives. He slams the demon box back into my hands and I cannot let go.

"I uh… But, er, mmm…" I stammer to let reaction catch up to the Devil. Suddenly I feel an ominous presence emanating from the box and it makes me nauseous. My world spins in the pull of a tornado. I fall to my knees, the box still stuck to my hands, trying to stay awake, but it is too much. Instead of vomiting profusely and seeing the Devil's smug grin curl up, I simply pass out.

Wake up with a splitting headache, even though I only had a sip. As you can imagine, that bastard got the better of me again, because I am lying on hard pavement. Redundant, I know. The stupid box is beside me, staring down with furrowing brows. Grabbing the box, I wonder if all the stress will lay barren my near-hairless scalp. I grab one of the two cars that surround and lift myself. As I figure, the "Sellebration." There are cars all over and for good reason too. Cheap deals at low, low prices going on in honor of the recently built third floor. Beyond this vast, shining metallic sea are people of every sort. Big, small, some with dogs, others without. Even a father with his own two boys.

Course he is also arm-and-arm with some woman who is probably not his backstabbing ex-wife, so I envy him a little.

These people are all carrying bags, sacks, totes; all full of merchandise. Trying to turn back and fight my contractual obligations does not seem to be effective, because the box is acting like a curious dog. It is sealing my hands and pulling me. Basically a person fighting with the pull of a semi at this point. Soon it feels like my motions are clockwork, beyond my control in all aspects but my thinking. Mmm, raspberry Schnapps. Weird time to consider it, I know, I just wonder if it had any hand in my mild resistance. I could really go for something to quench my terrible thirst, and I am not even thirsty.

I am not sure of the time as I begin to weave through groups of people. I do not wear a watch, but the sun looks to be around half past afternoon at least. Nobody thinks I look suspicious. A zombie holding a box and nobody notices him. Maybe it is all the eye-catching deals and *free* samples. I will not have to worry about such things when I am immortal. Most material things seem to lose meaning and efficiency when even rocks die off before the end.

It worries me, the subtle dark gaze of this box is deflecting sane logic from people staring right at me. Soon I shall know what is within. I leads me sniffing for the right spot, passing by the various shops selling electronics, wooden clocks, t-shirts, designers hoes, and other knick-knacks; until I stop in the most grandeur area of the mall. I am motionless; my body still in captivity. Standing like a gift-giving mannequin in all the shop windows. I see people bustling about in quite the hurry; some are slipping rudely by, mostly high-thrills teens. But directly in front, shining most gloriously under the skylight far above is a fountain. You think this could be it? What I have been going through to get? The Fountain of Youth, the artifact of legend sought by... Well, you know that uncivil Spanish guy. Name is not really important.

Here it is, hidden in a mall, laden with copper coins beneath constantly splashing water, with a pedestal holding a clock. The clock's face looks diamond-esque, shimmering under both the skylight and constantly adjusting reflections from the water. The clocks' face seems to also reflect and illuminate all the stores at various paces, and even lands on the box. It also makes it hard to read, the special fonts and reflecting light, but when focusing on the pale-green pole below it, I can sort of make out the time.

Twenty minutes to four. Wow, this stupid box kept me out long enough to keep from fooling around anymore. My body suddenly feels vastly heavier and I stumble. People stray away from me. They must think it is far too early in the afternoon, but it is not like that this time. Your body gets much heavier after parole from possession. Deciding to hold onto the box may be a bad idea, but I am already here. Living forever will get lonely, but at least I will be able to do enough to make the boys proud, help the world, and maybe even get an award or five. Perhaps the Devil's cruel tricks of suffering could be filled with card games. Yes, take up gambling. What is the worst that could happen? I lose my 401k? Ha ha. I slip the box under my arm and look back at the clock's round face. The clock is almost split down the middle. Ten minutes to. I hear the tick-tock in my mind, click-click-click. Strange for a clock to tick so loudly among the masses.

This is it though. Not the clock, something else tick-tocks. I realize the conclusion of this trap rapidly coming. Can you guess it? Mm-hmm, the box under my arm. I hold and rattle the demon box. The click-click-click becomes more consistent, louder, echoing inside my soul. Bouncing all around the court area I see the myriad shoppers, countless in their passing. And I notice the support beams near the wall, holding up the second and newly constructed third floor. Starting to shake at my realizations, I try to hasten my thoughts.

Instead I run. Suddenly all the lights spark out and darkness surrounds. This again. The darkness swells like a storm cloud at its peak and the place begins to smoke and decay at a rapid rate. The infestation comes. I pause in fear of such a horrible being, so vast in his power and see the deep-red eyes pierce through from the emptiness. The smoke's harsh nature takes on a wrinkly and sickly form, but nobody seems to move any quicker. Many shoppers pass through this thick cloud without attention. Can nobody see this? Can only I, the holder of the demon box? Lighting strikes somewhere because thunder hits me hard.

"Goin' sumwhere sir?" The cloud bellows and almost pushes me backward.

The cloud rumbles as it laughs, "Contract's a contract. 'Sides, everythin' you want's in tha box. You be 'live ferever in mind of the country." Finally he pauses and slows his speech. "Immortality is gifted to few."

"But why all these people!? Why not just me?"

He speeds up again, "Man' peop' owe me here. Others is ingredien' for powerfu' elix'. Take man' soul to keep one fresh. Think. Criminals here, look round. Is right thing."

"But-"

"No fight! Time to crea'." And with that the foulest of evil is so great around me that my skin starts to smolder where I grasp the box. I try to drop it, but it seals itself to my skin no matter where I hold it. Suspending itself from falling by attaching to my body. This foul darkness travels through my arms and stings my eyes, until it pollutes my brain. It feels like someone is mining syringes through my veins, my blood cells commit suicide before they feel the coming touch, and my hope dies.

After I finish feeling the sensation of devilish advocating fingers through my scalp I feel emptiness for these people. I relinquish myself to standing back at the fountain, my box sticking to one hand. Simply shall I stare at the clock and wait. At least they all get a rush of purchase before it happens. *Hurry, one day only.*

It seems I can feel them all, their lurking desires. Thinking of men in black and white striping shirts, carrying sacks with dollar signs. Others have scar-laden faces with pocketknives. I imagine even less inspiring thoughts, those of kids eating candy not theirs, pushing down the weaker ones. I think of women sneaking stuff into their pockets and business men overpricing. It all seems so pointless now.

The clock is but moments from the "Sellebration's" end. Guess the doors are closing early. I reach for my flask in my inner coat pocket, difficult because of only one free hand. I get a surprise from reflecting light. My face is struck by the clock's, and I drop the flask. My grip is none too powerful at this point. My nerve-calmer taps the ground and settles, and when I bend to pick it up, my eyes leave the clock and see only below it.

Around me are various smiling people. I see the man with scars and he is helping an old lady pick up her bags. She kind of looks like the Old Bag Lady on the bus in fact. There are plump ladies talking with each other and laughing about something or other. I even see the little kids on the wrist-leashes. I always find them a little cruel, but it keeps a lazy eye on the active sprouts. Even a discount I hear from a store owner nearby. I realize that even if they do things sinfully, they more than do righteous things to make up for it. Besides, my boys do not want to live in the shadow of their father. Constantly looked down on for a choice chosen, stuck in the muck of a father's past. And so once again the Devil proves wrong and deceiving, and I realize what must be done. What would you do?

Making use of my time now, not the potential of the future, I shout, "There's a bomb in here! A bomb!"

Some people freeze and yammer, other either do not hear or ignore me as a vagrant. I raise the box up and wave it as one would a flag. I stand on a bench next to the Fountain of Youth. "There is a bomb everyone! Look out! A bomb! A bomb!"

It must be the box that sets them off, because they all start screaming and running away from me. Some shield their children. Some even drop their merchandise to run faster. Finally! Finally everyone can see the box for what it is. Looks appealing on the outside, but who knows what is under the paper right? Oh geez! You still here? You better go, can you not hear the chimes? This must be the first one. Only five left before it is too late you know. Alright, stick around if you want, but it might get messy around here.

I step onto the ledge of the Fountain of Youth.

Chime

I look into the clear, fresh, burbling water below me. If I go, the Fountain of Youth is coming with, so that nobody else ever falls into the same trap.

Chime

I ready myself for the jump and wobble a bit before I forget. I reach for my wallet, which struggles against my pocket.

Chime

I pull the wallet out and look at the pictures of my boys in their little uniforms.

"Do not forget me Timmy and Tony. And hey, can you two at least remember the good times we had? Like the T-ball games and ninja fighting toys and that show you guys always talked about."

Chime

"Oh, have to hurry boys. I am going back to work. Guess I never could divorce it after all." I toss the wallet with all my strength and as I jump-

Chime

I hope my wallet lands a safe distance from the court area. I cannot tell because I am wrapping my body tightly into a cannonball form around the box, and I am holding it together with all my mortal might. A finite life tells me I have only one shot; my body a natural vice fighting an unbeatable box that begins to tear at the creases. The indestructible paper finally flies away and the box swells with the sulfur smell.

I cannot hold it any longer, but my body submerges. The box's contents expand to a size that grows too fast for such a container. My lungs quickly fill with the Fountain of Youth's fluids; the elixer of life drains from me just the same.

The sensation is so awkward. It is amazing how much time you get toward the very end. The molecules breaking and burning away sections of this body separating and moving everywhere, levitating, surging. Maybe I will be reborn anew. Not from ashes born, but from odors of raspberries. I can already smell it, fruit-heavy sulfur.

Just then, a hand as quick as a cobra, or maybe a mongoose, rips me from the shallow liquid with tile-floor.

"...Explosion, which witnesses say was the alleged result of a bomb, blew away smiling faces of happy consumers at the city's "Sellebration." They didn't think they would be having a sale on fearful tears. Police are still investigating, but they claim, reportedly, the brunt of the damage consumed only a minor part of the mall's court area, namely an exquisite fountain that was constructed in honor of the mall's third floor development. Thankfully no bodies were reported found, and so police are expecting a death toll of zero lives, pending the end of the investigation. Additionally, the police have not yet stated if they believe this to be an act of terrorism. Despite it all, surely we can all agree that this is a miracle and it makes this reporter, just a little, think there might be something protecting all of us out there. In other news today..."

Mr. Orator's Inescapable Conflict

Maverick crashed through the ceiling, rupturing a decently sized hole into the roof. The wood splintered like a light rainfall when Maverick finally crashed into the chair at the kitchen table. The chair bent a little, but only because the ceiling absorbed so much of the impact. He wobbled to regain his heroic composure, and collapsed his head depressingly in his hands. Maverick sat opposite Nate Orator who was likewise at the kitchen table trying to enjoy a bowl of instant oatmeal.

Maverick donned a domino mask with bright orange shoulder, elbow, and knee pads. The rest of his suit varied colors of red, making a flame-themed outfit. Nate Orator, somewhat less impressive, donned a ratty old bathrobe and comfy pleather loafers. Underneath that was an impressively crisp white t-shirt and canvas shorts, where one would assume a man has to have style somewhere.

So there Mr. Orator was, trying to read his paper, and spooning gobs of sloppy oatmeal into his mouth, mashing away at still crystallized brown sugar he always poured on top. He squinted, looked up from his paper at the depressed Maverick, looked down at his paper, and then folded it lightly off to the side. He continued to munch his oatmeal until he was scraping the bottom of the ceramic bowl for more brown sugar; Maverick looked on the whole time.

"The roof was just fixed Mr. Maverick. You use the front door every other time, but as soon as I pay the ungodly repair bill, you break more of my shingles. As if the housing market was not bad enough already," Mr. Orator said calmly with cool eyes. He put his hands up as though ending his disappointment and smirked heartily. "No matter. It is indeed a relaxing Sunday, and I'm not standing for any trouble today. Going to sit in my bathrobe and, well, I suppose I will just sit in my bathrobe."

Maverick lifted his head from the cradle of hands, "Don't you want to hear about why I crashed through the roof?"

"I said I was not to have any trouble today. I get maybe two days off every three or four months, and I don't want to bother it up with what I deal with day in and out. Trouble. No trouble, no worries, no frustration, sadness, petty love affairs, or lost mystical rubies. But most of all, no conflict!" Mr. Orator had a knack for trouble, always had, and he made a damn good living off it. He was a very popular character, and the more epic the venture, the more often he got another letter in the mail, or knock at his chamber door. In the end though, sometimes a man has to rest and be alone with himself.

And so the two sat in more silence, Mr. Orator with every limb folded and crossed, Maverick sitting, tapping his fingertips. The breeze was light through the house, courtesy of the hole in the ceiling that whistled deeply. Soon Maverick opened his mouth again, "Had some oatmeal hmm?"

"Indeed I did," Mr. Orator said without opening his eyes. He breathed deeply as though he were passing to sleep.

"Good stuff, good stuff. I like the apple cinnamon kind best."

"Reasonable tastes you have."

"Yeah, I'd have had some this morning, but boy," Maverick leaned back in the chair and rocked it on the back two legs as he looked into the sky through the ceiling's hole, "I was so entangled with Monsieur Moth, French burglar extraordinaire. Didn't have the time. Now breakfast is over, so what's the point? Yep, Monsieur Moth sure is hard to fight alone, need teamwork I swear."

Mr. Orator opened his eyes and furrowed his brows, "Listen *friend*, I know what you're getting at, and I don't see how I am of much help. Like Jimmy Olsen to Superman, I am little more than backup. You are the one with superpowers, your flight and flame abilities. In fact, Monsieur Moth is a giant moth, a moth my friend. Surely you could lure him in with a candle or torch." With that Mr. Orator pushed the chair away from the table and retired to his living room.

He was among the grandeur trinkets that were mounted on the walls and mantle. He poked a fire awake in his smoky fireplace with a fine steel fire-poker. He sauntered to the couch also laden with various trinkets. He picked up blueprints and maps to Noah's Ark, a fossilized arm of Vishnu, several glowing tarot cards and a small spade.

He sat down and let out a hushed, panged tone. He rubbed his bottom while taking off a couch cushion. With two hands he dragged out a large tooth from a leviathan which had a "thank you" note inscribed on it from a Mr. Geppetto. He placed it on the solid oak coffee table which buckled lightly under the weight. Out from the couch also came a small cardboard box wrapped in tamper-proof tape. Seemingly unimpressive, this certain cardboard box contained the entire contents of reality as man knew it. Where it to be opened, the entire fabric of reality would tear and pour out, overlapping the reality it contained which would create a veritable hell.

Mr. Orator slipped on bifocals to inspect the package, "So this is where I put that old thing." He tossed the box over his shoulder and it bounced against the granite mantle. There was a miniature earthquake which settled when the box stopped rolling. Mr. Orator delved deep into the couch and pulled out several nickels, dimes, gold doubloons, and even a quarter. He bounced the change in his hand satisfied and slipped the money into his pocket, replacing the couch cushion.

"Figure I'll go back out and find that Monsieur Moth," Maverick shouted from the kitchen.

Mr. Orator adjusted himself until he found a comfortable position to sit, propping his feet upon the solid oak table which bended under the further weight, making a dipping curved shape, "Suit yourself."

Maverick hesitated, but eventually made way into the living room where he sat on an adjacent chair, "Course, the wind is a little rough right now. Might not be safe to fly. A little chilly too. You have a scarf around here?"

"No, I find them lacking style," Mr. Orator said reaching into a torn pocket of his bathrobe which his hand went through completely. "Hmm, house keys were in there. I'll have to look for them later."

"Well, guess I'll get going. Sure hope I don't catch hypothermia out there."

"I know what you are getting at Mr. Maverick. I find it acceptable to stay here, if for a short while, but don't tease my intellect into pity when you can set your body aflame."

Maverick leaned back in the leather chair and scratched lightly at its cracking hide, "Say, this leather from the discarded hides of Ganesha?"

"Sure is, glad you recognize it. Yes, I helped Brahma out of another mess, when he granted a boon to some eternal demon, and in their reincarnations some of the gods sent me gifts. I got a really big suit from Ganesha, pure leather. Instead of cutting it down I wrapped it around some couches and chairs I got when I traveled back in time." Mr. Orator picked up a blue-tinged arm, "And that is also the story of how I got this fabulous backscratcher."

Maverick had been ignoring Mr. Orator, more interested in turning on the telly. He placed his finger over the button, and a whack released it. "Ow! What the heck? I was only going to watch the news. I'm a goddamned superhero you know."

"That may be, but you are a guest in my house, my friend, and I will not stand to have my day off ruined with conflicts either childish or world-threatening. No murders, thefts, atomic warfare, death tolls, leukemia walks, or the like. No overly salty brownies at the bake sale, no wrong change, no lonely pups for adoption, and especially, especially no potential desires to call a pizza delivery boy and wait out a hunger. Basically, my friend... No, Mr. Maverick, I do not, on today of all days, wish to deal with any trouble! I want today to be uneventful, plain, boring even. I don't want a rush of excitement, I don't want the anxious feeling of trying to solve a problem. I want to sit here! Let us play cards, fine. Risky as it is, fine, but if you have but an ounce of respect for what little solidly sane course of thought I maintain, no television please!" Mr. Orator stopped his berated barrage and wiped clean the saliva building around the corner of his mouth.

There was an awkward silence afterward. Maverick really wanted to know the weather, but he didn't want to make a move for the newspaper in the kitchen. He glanced around the living room for a short while taking in Nate Orator's vast collection. He saw various scraps of paper around the chair, as well as a half-full pot of coffee, which still seemed close to half full. He finally cleared his throat, "So what do you want to do? I know, how about Chinese checkers?"

"Regular checkers suppose I can manage."

The board was set, Mr. Orator red and Maverick black. Maverick took first move into a safe border position; Mr. Orator took a quick shot at moving his piece toward the center, a bold advance so early on. The two played for some time, an old wooden grandfather clock made them each aware of every second that passed in their concentrated game.

Maverick broke the silence, "So Nate, how do you plan on keeping potential clients from seeking your help?" Maverick moved his piece into a key position on the board, but the red pieces had already made it there. "You are, after all, the best consultant for those seeking greatness. You've helped tons of people cut their losses and increase renown-revenue."

Mr. Orator chuckled, "Poor move Mr. Maverick," He jumped a black piece and claimed it with the small pile on his side of the table. He was moving for a king spot. "But, since you asked, I will be so kind as to tell you. I have taken certain foresights in regards to my desire to avoid conflict and relax my day away. I powered down all communication devices in my abode, and dismantled those I couldn't. I made sure not to leave the house, it was trouble enough to even grab the newspaper this morning, but I so do love my jumbles. The last resort is my top of the line security system to ward off trespassers. This is an impenetrable fortress."

"Really? What kind of security system? Lasers, gas canisters, maybe a cloaking shell?" Maverick questioned when he jumped three pieces in succession.

Mr. Orator scoffed and leaned forward rapidly scanning the board. One hand gripped the table, while his other hand shakily reached for a red piece. He picked it up and rotated it slowly in his hands until a light coat of sweat moistened it. He rubbed the red piece on his tattered bathrobe and slowly lowered it toward a space deeper into black's territory. Suddenly that same hand knocked all the pieces, black and red, asunder, soaring toward the fireplace, where one or two pieces rolled. Maverick's hands were lightly patting the table, like a blind man trying to find his walking stick. Mr. Orator was the barking dog to guide his vision.

"I cannot handle the conflict dear friend! I had to end the game when I became frustrated with my hasty movements. Surely you understand."

"C'mon, I almost had that game. Red was on the ropes. You Nate, are a poor sport. Why I haven't had a game like that since Dralette and I played Monopoly. I almost had her after a two day game, but as per her usual tricky ways, she made me think I was winning while trapped in a dream. I woke up and not only were my little red hotels and green houses gone, she took my wallet. Fraud protection tracked her expenses somewhere in Ecuador. I didn't even know they took credit cards out there!"

"Why did I have to be red? I am not the one with the majestic flame suit." Mr. Orator sighed, "I am most sorry friend. Let us not fight. I know, let us play the Bone Trade. It's a marvelous game I learned when living in the dark reaches of Africa. There was a tribe who lived in a forever shaded region of the rainforest; they played this game where you trade back and forth any number for any number, long as you left one bone for the other player."

"I don't get it. How do you win?"

"Now you have spied the wondrous thing about this tribe. They were heavenly peaceful. They didn't believe in fun found in making a loser of someone. There is never an end to the game," Mr. Orator's lips peeled back into an overly joyous gleam, "Except when you laughed so hard you couldn't hold your bones. I once made a pun regarding funny bones, and the people of the tribe found it quite humorous. Pity though, they never went to war and were wiped out due to overpopulation." Mr. Orator stood from the couch and walked, hands together, toward a fastened skeletal structure. Held together with various bolts and twine was the skeleton of a manticore. Its body similarly shaped like a lion was a nice choice for large bones, and the three rows of razor teeth would make for numerous small trades. He left the scorpion-esque tail alone because it was still highly venomous even in death. With a stack of bones Mr. Orator turned around, with light-hearted step, when he saw Maverick.

Maverick was holding a pot of coffee, almost half-filled to Maverick, but it was roughly half-emptied when Mr. Orator looked on. There were small vapors of steam seeping from the container, clearly heated by a white-hot flame from Maverick's hand, as he poured the coffee into a large cup on the coffee table.

"No you fool!" Finally the weight of objects grew too heavy for the shoulders of the table and it split in two, the legs cracking off in the impact. Various documents and trinkets clunked to the floor, which were shattered under the heavier Leviathan tooth. The cup slid from the edge before Maverick could grab it, and the brownish-red liquid splashed to the floor around the breaking point. The coffee smelled lightly of roses, which the red-tinge reflected.

Mr. Orator shuffled without sound to Maverick, whom he grabbed tightly by the collar. Naturally, being of fire borne, Maverick's body was of unusually high temperature, which reflected in the bulbous blisters of Mr. Orator's hands that recoiled. They didn't smell quite like roses. "Why did you pour coffee into the grail?"

"The grail? I thought it was a cappuccino mug."

"You thought *the* grail was a cappuccino mug!" Maverick and Mr. Orator stopped their arguing when they heard *shplop, slpork, squush-squush.* Maverick was already looking on; Mr. Orator turned slowly round. At the collapsed broken point, where the leviathan tooth laid, dripping with reddish-black coffee from the large cup, there were stringy tendons quickly shooting out and rapidly tying themselves around into solid muscles. Flesh grew atop, expanding as more mass collected from nowhere.

"Hurry my friend, we must dispose of this quickly!" Mr. Orator grabbed one end of the tooth, while Maverick grabbed the gooey, evolving side. He tried to burn away some chunks of meat, but they grew back just as quick. Soon his hands were being enveloped in the solidifying fishy substance. The two carried the tooth as quickly as they could back to the kitchen, but the thing's weight kept on multiplying. With just enough effort they rocked the thing back and forth until they released it, smashing through the kitchen window, where the quivering mass bounced and twisted on the ground as more pieces assembled.

Baby teeth sprouted from the mass of gums and quickly aged to a lightly cracked, fully grown leviathan tooth. When the large jaw had formed itself, the skin started unrolling over what would become the belly of the beast, and soon enough, rolls of other flesh covered that one, ribs burst through the skin like loaded springs. The outer layer of flesh inflated as though it were being filled with a fine wine, blood. This creature was now more like a water-balloon, its shape quickly filling out and consuming the spacious backyard.

Mr. Orator's tree that grew golden apples was timbered, a beanstalk snapped and recoiled quickly into the sky like a severed bridge cable, but not before it grounded a valuable faberge egg collection to fine powder, which Mr. Orator had been meaning to move inside. And when the tail fin was full and mighty, it slammed down on a garden of morning glories and moon flowers. The holes in the outer layer of skin sealed as they passed the ribs, and two large slits formed above the mouth cavity. These slits ripped open with the sound of torn sheets and there the leviathan lay complete and alive.

It looked enraged at first, as though engaged in battle, but ended confused when its eyes rolled around to see no fierce naval battle, but calm, cleanly cut grass with a wooden privacy fence nearby. The leviathan tried to push itself along, but dug itself deeper into soft earth. It flapped its fins back and forth in a panic, but it was no good, the leviathan was far too heavy. The creature, despite being large beyond reason, looked with full soft eyes inside the house. It moaned deeply, echoing into the distance.

Mr. Orator sighed and retreated back into the living room. He pulled out a bottle of aloe from his other intact bathrobe pocket and rubbed his singed hands.

"Don't you think it's kind of strange to keep a bottle of Aloe in your bathrobe?" Maverick had followed Mr. Orator back into the room.

"I see my friend, the bottle of Aloe is what is strange. Never mind the leviathan you brought to life in my backyard. Thank goodness for privacy fences. Neighbors would have my head. Already have a citation for keeping too much of my collection in the yard. Now I suppose it doesn't matter," Mr. Orator paused and considered the next course of discussion, "No bother, I will worry about troublesome things tomorrow, I still have at least half a day left to relax. What was it you asked again?"

"I suppose it really isn't important. I don't see people carrying Aloe with them wherever they go is all."

"I am a planner Mr. Maverick. I plan constantly and prepare myself for any situation. One gains incredible insight when they stick with the business as long as I. One such step of planning happens to be aloe, in case my hands get burned, and viola, it all makes sense."

Mr. Orator and Maverick spoke of the matter of the leviathan. Mr. Orator had contemplated lighting up his pipe. He was not an avid smoker by any means, but it had been long since he filled his pipe made of ivory and onyx. A weighty tool, but relaxing still. It only came to him because of the reflections he saw on the nearby window Maverick was closest too. The window seemed to carry a light noise on its fragile frame, a clanking sound, aluminum against aluminum.

"The security system is going off. Looks like someone was foolish enough to test it after all."

"Security system? It sounds like a bunch of old cans tied together."

"I certainly was not going to recycle them!" Mr. Orator slinked over to the front door and peeked through the peephole. He looked around relieved to see no one there. He still had a lot of conflict to avoid by the end of the day; he did not need any more unexpected guests. His security system was AWOL, but Mr. Orator assumed it may have been the wind or an animal frightened off with them. He turned around to see Maverick, good old Maverick; beside him a girl in black, good old girl in black. Mr. Orator did a double-take when he saw her there. He tested the locks, seemed fine, turned back, she was still there.

She was drabbed in black and deep gray cloth, Mr. Orator clearly made out an extra-short mini-skirt that was more of a façade to style than it was to pragmatism. Underneath were loose-fitting leg warmers with bright orange fuzzies stuck to them. She had on two different colored socks on top of those, as well as Japanese-styled solid wood sandals which she was clopping around mildly.

For one reason or another she found it a stylistic choice to wear a black shawl over a black angora sweater over a gray tank top, the strap of which was barely visible through the mess. Adorning all was a string of empty tin cans strewn together. The most distracting thing to Mr. Orator's eye, however, was her long bleach-blonde hair, which while not that unusual, was completely spiked upward, as though defying simple physics. She stopped bouncing on her sandals and leaned forward to stare deeply into Mr. Orator's eyes, her thick, thick mascara shadowing most every other feature on her face.

"Heeeey there," She balanced on one leg and turned almost completely upside-down as she gazed ever deeper into the window of Mr. Orator's soul. "Hmm. Reasons come here there were, yep yep. Can't remember, maybe me is incomplete."

"Don't pull that on us!" Maverick lashed his arm out and his suit started to flutter and wave, the air around him steamed with it, the flames were coming. "You owe me six houses and three hotels!"

So this was the trickster Dralette, apprentice to the queen of dreams. She reached inside her shawl and dropped several red and green plastic pieces into Maverick's hand. Unfortunately for Maverick, he was still in fury, and so were his flames, which easily melted the plastic houses.

"Oh no, Baltic Avenue, you were the most underrated of my property."

"Houses only taken because men of flame no no need them,"

"Devil queen!"

"Matchstick."

"Why I oughta…"

"Hold, Mr. Maverick! I won't have you burning down another house," Mr. Orator didn't quite mean it like that, the orphanage was a touchy subject to Maverick, but he managed to cool his flames anyway. "So, Ms. Dralette, what brings you all the way from the land of dreams? It is not but half past three, surely the land of dreams cannot break through the walls of our world until nightfall."

"Woooow, impressive, already names knowing, tease. They said he good, they be right. But Dralette no is of pure dream energy, only one who messenger could be."

"They? Ms. Dralette, whatever problems face you will have to be gone alone by your own people. I am officially on vacation."

"But biggin beast coming," Started shaking her arms frantically, "really, really big beast. Horns growing through clouds and snort shoot, shoot, shooting out. Many a dream man blown to dust. Only made of simple dream energy, not much against growing biggin beast. Maybe work together we pullin' the nose ring. Draggin' the beast through before is fully grown. People need sleep, we provide the wonder, and we feast on the desires of, hey, what's that?"

Mr. Orator turned calmly in his tattered bathrobe and smiled, "Ah that, my dear Dralette, is a map of Utopia. A fairly basic place of humble means, you may have heard it called by many names. The Land of Paradise, Heaven, perhaps even Eden. All are good names. I traveled but once there, but have never found readmission, for it quickly fades from sight. Everything serene would be subject to chaos if it stayed in one spot for but a blink of an eye. The Brigadoon of my heart, a place without those troubles and conflicts. Much as they make my life, they break it as well. So you see Ms. Dralette, thus is one of my most prized…" Mr. Orator turned back around and saw Ms. Dralette, with her long, spiked, bleach-blonde hair standing there, innocent as could be, tip-toeing slowly toward the door, her clothes bulging with various treasures. Map tubes jutted out from under her shawl, tops and experimental candy poked out of unknown pockets, and she was even carrying away part of the manticore skeleton only recently dismantled.

Maverick gasped and looked from side to side, "She tricked us with her disgusting dream magic again. You'll pay Dralette, you'll pay!" Maverick was shaking his fist toward where the land of dreams supposedly resided, staying near the dark side of the moon. Apparently, Maverick could not see her, despite how obvious her escape. Mr. Orator walked dignified to the door and flipped a latch. Hands full, Dralette, apprentice to the queen of dreams herself, was trapped.

"You seeing me? Woooow, you even better than 'fore. Dream magic supposed to affect anything."

"I can tell," Mr. Orator said while grabbing the treasures back from Dralette as well as his sophisticated series of tin cans she was wrapped in, "You being not of complete dream energy are likewise affected, which is why you should one day seriously consider the consequences of kleptomania. As for me, when you have seen almost everything, fared virtually every task, there is not much left to dream about."

"That why you be helping the dreamers. You one of only people can slow the biggin beast."

"I am sorry Ms. Dralette, but not today. Maybe tomorrow, maybe next week, maybe hours after the stroke of midnight, but not today. I, Nate Orator, by my solemn word, have chosen to forgo the challenging scenarios and the intensity of thought. I don't want to deal with the conflict! So Ms. Dralette, I advise your precocious nature to be of enough merit to," He paused. "Do you hear rhythmic gusts of wind?"

Dralette followed Mr. Orator as he made haste to the window where Maverick was literally steaming. Freed of illusion Maverick sensed the danger, ceased anger, and took up the mantle of heroism as the three collectively peered out the window skyward. Flapping its mighty wings and fluttering high in the sky was a gigantic moth. Its segmented eyes were drawn altogether at a powerful flame it sensed, and it was pushing against the house with the full of its weight. The housed rocked against the leviathan outside who moaned and pushed it back, until soon the house was a ship on rocky seas.

"Let's roll gang!" Maverick made the signal and the two followed closely behind him up the stairs, which Dralette paused just long enough to admire the sparkly banister adorned with various carvings along the rails. On the second floor they ran to Mr. Orator's main chambers, where he would lay his head to rest.

Wood began splintering, the house creaked, and the ceiling
churned until it split. Chunks of wood fell the ground, Mr.
Orator standing agape as his main chamber's ceiling was torn
free by the giant moth. The gigantic moth looked intrigued, as
well as a gigantic moth could looked intrigued, and started
lowering as gusts of wind almost blew the group of three over.

"No, not that," Mr. Orator saw what the gigantic moth
sought, and he broke a run for it. He only managed to make it to
his bedpost before he had to grip tight, because a powerful
vacuum started lifting his dressers and wardrobes, each as heavy
as a bolder. They started to lift off the ground, Mr. Orator tightly
holding to his bedpost, as the drawers and doors pulled open,
legions of fabric flying upward into the maw of the gigantic
moth. Its hungry chewing could be heard, like a man chewing on
a piece of straw, as it feasted on Mr. Orator's supply. The
furniture pieces fell back to the floor when the wind subsided.
The floor cracked and large holes remained underneath, potholes
in a home.

"Monsieur Moth, you fiend!" Maverick struck when the
wind was weakest. He took flight; his suit flickered as the flame
designs came forward and burst into flames. They struggled in
great battle in the sky as Mr. Orator and Dralette looked on
through the new skylight. Maverick shot flames at Monsieur
Moth as it fluttered on a draft, full and satisfied. Monsieur Moth
easily dodged the flames, and a wing slapped Maverick back,
singeing its wings. This continued on for several more moments
until Monsieur Moth fell back and created a strong windfall that
sent paralyzing poison sailing through the air; however, being of
flame borne, Maverick grew stronger against the influx of
oxygen. A giant fireball in the sky, Mr. Orator started to sweat
under the heat and his bed began to smolder.

Maverick shot a column of flame, striking true into
Monsieur Moth. A chitterling sound burst through it, the
antennae shaking in reaction to the pain. Monsieur Moth
fluttered carelessly around with a newly charred puncture and
singed wings. Finally it crashed into Mr. Orator's remaining

ceiling which collapsed with Monsieur Moth. It lay there sputtering and convulsing its body until finally it coughed up a gooey gray substance that oozed onto Mr. Orator's recently polished hardwood floor, already coated with fine chunks of paralyzing powder. Maverick's flame disbursed.

"You guys alright?"

"Mr. Maverick, I would… Never mind, I am immune to such things, that is all that needs to be said."

"Dralette over seventy percent dream energy. Problems no," Dralette flexed her frail arms. She started to imitate Maverick shooting flame and made the appropriate sound effects, "Shoo shoo. Shooting good hot-head."

"Don't put this all on me, stupid. I might have gotten a lucky shot in, but Monsieur Moth is tougher than that," He looked back at the ooze dripping out of the mandibles of the deceased creature, "Something tells me the high heat sped up the eventual."

"I can attribute to that Mr. Maverick," Mr. Orator dusted the paralyzing powder off the old bathrobe, "Moth balls. I told you a man of my position is prepared for anything. Speaking of which…" Mr. Orator looked at a clock with a now broken face when a gutturally intense moan poured through the house into the city streets.

"What that?"

"Nate, don't tell me-"

"Tell you what my friend? That I would let the mighty leviathan suffer until death lying in my yard? I don't think so. I am by no means brutal. A mercy killing is what it defines. As for the moth, well, trespassing *is* illegal." Maverick and Dralette gulped and took a step back together. The group shortly heard a splorching, a squirtch, and a bloop several times, when they found the source of the sound.

Next to Monsieur Moth were five slimy moth larvae, roughly the size of a full-grown Doberman, inching around, feeling the dirty floor and the fur of their deceased parent.

"Well I'll be, Monsieur Moth was actually a Madame!" Maverick said as he picked up a slimy baby. "To think, another couple of days and the entire countryside would be plagued by these things. Still, without a mother, what are we going to do with these things?"

"Food ready almost!" Yelled Dralette.

"Ms. Dralette, I appreciate the concern, but there are only three of us present. How is the meal coming along?"

"Going great, that smoky flavor is going to be so imbedded we're going to think there's fire in our bellies. And the natural juices of the barbeque are a grand addition to the flavor." Maverick was blasting his barbeque pit, the leviathan, with powerful flame jets. In addition to being a hero, he was also a star grill-master.

Before Maverick was the mighty leviathan, recently deceased. There was dark, strong-smelling smoke pouring out of an open wound in the roof of the sea-creature's skull. The central object protruding from the leviathan was a sword that even the tallest of giants would have trouble handling.

Massively large, it dwarfed Mr. Orator's grandiose abode, which one could easily mistake for a mansion. The blade gleamed brightly against the setting sun, and the metal was never touched but for now. Up the blade which extended far off into the sky and almost through the clouds was the hilt, decorated with precious metals and gems larger than found in any record book. There too the carvings gave way to something mysterious, which overshadowed even the jewels that formed it. Tied to the shaft was a very large and bulky beanstalk, girth wider than a sycamore. On the tip of the handle, where placed was a symbol of hope, there was also a small blinking red light no larger than a beach ball to warn low flying planes. Mr. Orator had found the light discarded among junk in a back closet; Maverick had placed the thing up there.

Mr. Orator wouldn't talk about where he got the sword. Said he got it a long time ago from an acquaintance of his. A friend of his, named Jack, had given him a seed to plant, a gardening fiasco, but it proved the perfect place to hang the sword. Mr. Orator, after all, was prepared anything. When questioned further, he couldn't explain how he was prepared for his ceiling caving in, or how he would dispose of Madame Moth's carcass, but dinner was almost ready and that was fine enough for the other two.

Maverick pulled five well-done, yet tender, slabs from the smoky cavern of the leviathan's mouth and placed the plate at the table. Dralette had made rainbow-colored corn-on-the-cob in the kitchen, but Mr. Orator couldn't enjoy it, for it was a product of dream energy, so it appeared an empty plate. They also had to eat with their hands, because all the silverware mysteriously disappeared from the kitchen when Dralette jingled her way outside.

The food was all placed out; the sky a magnificent array of colors that signaled the coming of nightfall. Mr. Orator leaned onto the picnic table and released, "I cannot take it. I cannot! It's my vacation today, I was supposed to relax, but instead it was more packed with action than, than, urrgh. I wanted to avoid it all. To live my life, for but one day, to sip soothe-berry iced tea and be absent of trouble, dissention, work, hostility, rancor, oppugnancy, competitions, contention, contradistinction, and most all conflict!" Mr. Orator dropped the thesaurus from his hands.

"Maybe in your tries at stopping conflict, you just ended up in more. Perhaps by avoiding trouble, you are creating conflict for yourself no matter what. And maybe, just maybe, all the trouble and conflict is necessary for us to survive, to keep away from the greater problems in life." There was a moment of silence as Maverick began doling out the servings on the plates.

"Dralette agree, it fun getting into trouble."

"My dear friend, I understand your deep desires in which to maintain your heroic standpoint by providing a moral, but consider the necessity. Have I not gone through enough today in which to determine such things? I am merely stating I want a day without having to worry about house repair. Also, can you please turn that thing off? It is giving me a headache."

Maverick frowned and flicked off a tape recorder playing sentimental music from the latter part of an episode of *Saved by the Bell*, "A hero has to have some standards."

There was an awkward silence for some time after, but soon all was well again, and Mr. Orator regaled Maverick and Dralette with various exploits involved in the process of his career until nightfall, but many stories fell from significance because Dralette needed them explained numerous times.

As Mr. Orator was mid-chew, greasy fingers in air, small morsels spitting forth as he garbled through a full mouth, he noticed a glass of water rippling. This concern heightened when the plates started to rattle, until the ground was pounding with such force that plants in the yard began to uproot, and the sword lodged in the skull of the leviathan was dangerously close to shaking loose. The earthquake heightened as the ground ruptured and cracked as did dry and vast deserts. As tectonic plates shifted they saw large cloud puffs snorting forward against the moonlit sky and obscured starlight.

Mr. Orator's privacy fence shattered on the north side, and the pieces of wood propelled at such a pace as to impale the surrounding trees deeply. One such plank jettisoned so close to Mr. Orator that he received a burn from the intense friction surrounding the air. Gripping his face, he stood displeased to see his rude guest, bathrobe flowing in the bursts of wind that approached with steam clouds. The steam smelled of saliva and sweat, the origins of which Maverick discerned to be of beast nature.

When the clouds dispersed to enough clarity, before them was a massive ox of enough stature to shadow over old Blue of Paul Bunyan fame. The ox looked down upon them with its piercing eyes which glowed dimly red over the yard. Its horns gleamed of pure white and sharpest tack atop its head; the snout held within the mass of flesh, between nostrils, a doorknocker to the gates of the cosmos. The front fur was of darkest brown, but along the spine and ribs a sparkling purple flaked off as had the paralyzing powder from Madame Moth. At the flanks and length of tail were the remnants of clouds most mystical in nature. Mr. Orator knew immediately what he saw.

"Ms. Dralette," Mr. Orator said whilst rubbing his temples, "When you said a 'biggin beast' was breaking through the land of dreams, it would have been nice to know that what we were discussing was a behemoth!"

"No is male moth, he big, biggin beast. Told you hefty nose ring hanging down all droopy, but no believe Dralette," She said this waggling her finger with a condescending tone.

The behemoth was hoofing at the ground in a grand upheaval; each snort pushed upward the solidly cosmic nose-ring, where it thudded back on the spongy flesh of the snout. It lowered its head, and the horns steadied themselves on a broad-shouldered body.

Mr. Orator folded his arms and sneered arrogantly. He shook his head several times and chuckled, "This behemoth does not know what it is up against. Looks like we have to do the only logical thing."

Maverick stepped up, his arms burning bright, his ambitions brighter, "That's right! He may be inexplicably large; he may be even capable of breaking the barriers of thought into reality, along with hoofs of diamond defense easily tearing apart even granite stone with but a thoughtless touch. However, we are of far greater strength together! With fire, ingenuity, and dreamful hopes, nothing can stop the most powerful thing of all: teamwork! If this is our last stand, let us die legends in the minds of the people. Let us hold back this foul demon for but until night's end, whereupon our valor will inspire the resilience of the people, and strike down the courage of our irredeemably strong foe! Isn't that right Nate!" The sound of wooden clops and loafer flops were slowly decreasing in volume behind Maverick when he turned around to see the two sprinting off into the dark, Maverick was lit up like a powerfully distracting flare.

"Sorry my friend, but the interpretation was to run away to live and fight another day! Good luck, surely your headstone will be the obelisk of courageous souls long abandoned!" Mr. Orator waved wildly as his voice faded with footfall.

The behemoth charged.

Maverick backed up and all the fire around him sparked in fear as he looked for a perfect tool. As the behemoth grew larger in perception, so too did the worry in Maverick's heart. He took a defensive pose in his mind for but a thought, when only a shrug could grace his form. Maverick took to the sky and with a puffed match's flame was rocketed beyond the beast toward Mr. Orator and Dralette whereupon his speech smoked, "This is way too much trouble!"

The Day Music Returned

       In the times of Dark, in the distant future, there was a subtle change that soon created vast oppression. The people dulled and lazed toward their new thoughts. It happened on a level so miniscule that no one, sans those artsy college kids sipping their chai-tea and adjusting their thrift-store berets, noticed. Unfortunately, those same artsy college kids were too high to raise a fuss, and so the Chinchilla Rockets, Electric Eiffel Towers, and Johnny Racketbombers of the world perished.

       It all started deep in the Pacific Ocean several hundred years before the event. From the darkest depths from within cracks on the ocean floor to even darker regions, pitch black truly became known. A landmass rose, gently, softly, from those depths and emerged by rupturing the ocean floor. This eruption of new land created a tidal wave that surged forth across the ocean, but it was far too distant from any inhabited island to catch the brunt. The islands caught up contained barely a bird or two and perhaps a sea-borne turtle. Those miniscule islands were swallowed wholly, and the pillars they rested on cracked and splintered until these tiny islands collapsed back to the ocean floor, more rubble to scavenge for the beasts below.

       This new island made brief international news, but its lack of greenery and uselessness of location pushed the greedy desires of countries aside. And so that island sat, with the numerous species of fish that came from the depths with it. And with their new way of life, came new forms. Within only those hundreds of years, they grew legs, grew hunched, and eventually took their latest form in that of a humanoid. They had grayish-brown skin, like the color of their island. Their bodies were marked with covered scars of gills long since unused, garish leathery skin covered their sinisterly-obese minds that were continually advancing beyond their bodies. They covered their frail, yet tough, forms with tattered cloths found floating by in the ocean.

When they questioned the odd birds in the sky, and where the cloth was coming from, along with the cans, and other interesting trinkets, they theorized places that dwarfed their own cramped living spaces. With intense desires their mind's eye flared, and that burning curiosity boiled the water beneath their feet, creating a light steam that their nimble and frail frames wobbled on. Their eyes set toward the vast expanse of ocean that lay before them, and they traveled. Soon they met landmasses hundreds, thousands of times larger than their quaint place. And upon these landmasses were people tired from a long day. A day that involved many countries and thinning numbers. On this day the people were far too exhausted to raise their hands to hold back these gray-skinned floaters. Even if they had, their country would have collapsed, just like every other.

Within a short span of only ten years, these gray-skinned creatures had taken hold. They quickly grasped onto the concept of politics, but they found the methods too slow, and so with their laws enacted, they proceeded to the viciousness of brutal mental warfare. Their mind's eye glowed too brightly, and from that eye came something to be feared. Illusions were but a mere gesture of thought, as was the ability to move objects without touch, and to scream a horrible guttural sound similar to what an impaled, roasted fish would make. That scream echoed in the minds of the people and soon they laid down what little weapons they had. These gray-skinned creatures took up a new moniker, they became the Controllers.

They named themselves so because of a simple device found on many nations. A small rectangular item, generally a dulled silver, which seemed to bend a larger cube object to its bidding, without laying a hand on it. The Remote Controllers became too contrived, and so the shortened version was birthed, for they ruled over the people from their cities far from human travel.

Their cities built near Sri Lanka, for it reminded them of home. And from that home they constructed vastly technological structures, as well as robots to accomplish their bidding. The robots soon flooded out from the Controllers' cities and constructed as their masters saw fit. The electronic technology of the people dismantled, skyscrapers torn down in thunderous crashes, and worst of all, the removal of creation.

Granted, the people still came, the Controllers were not foolish enough to make them infertile, but another sort of creation was perhaps the people's greatest tool. The Controllers had seen the results. They had seen the tanks, guns, and explosives. Clever, but not more than something smarter still. The results were found in museums and concert halls. Pictures with paint that tasted horrible, non-living bodies forever stuck in strange positions, and the most worrisome to Controllers: music. Visual art, powerful as it was, could be limited or collected. Anyone could make music to inspire and move the people to action. And so the Controllers made their wise move. They silenced it.

A strict ban was placed on instruments, and soon those sad riffs, excited chords, and raged tunes grew sickly and died a painful death. Music vanished from the lands and soon the sickeningly dull elevator muzak took its place. And not 200 years later the people sit in structures similar to cottages of old, occasionally attending the pubs, and paying mental tributes to the robot avatars of the Controllers, with their same muzak tunes playing lightly through the shabby radios.

Hope was dead. All seemed to be bathed in the grayish color of the Controller's skin, and their fishy minds viewed content the lands below as they sat in stagnant rule.

It doesn't end there. Oh no. What would be the point to tales of futures to come if they provided nothing? And that is where, 200 years into the Controllers' rule, that our hero was finally overdue.

The rain fell gently, and in this particular village, the people were holing themselves away in the pub. The new generations had forgotten what their parents said of music, and sat dreamily listening to the crackling, mind-numbing muzak that churned out of the radio. Music a myth at this time, discussions of genre existed no more. Instead the people slowly slid their finger around the condensation built up around their stouts. The candles which lit the area bounced and flickered to the lulls of the conversation. One man in particular placed down another weighty coin and a new stout took its place. He pulled the glass close to him; a trail of light followed, until it dimly gleamed from the bar.

The rain had let up, time to return to work. They built stacks of material, for whatever purpose, and new stacks replaced them. Little did these people know of the Controllers' plan to keep the people in continual work, for in another plant some countries away, the people dismantled the objects built and placed them onto stacks, which were shipped off for whatever purpose.

The group of workers had the appearance of 19th century paper boys, but with less color, and their eyes drooped heavier than their paper bags. One gentleman, in fact, almost bumped into the Patrol. A legion of robots dispatched short years after the Controller's took hold, to keep the people in line, and terminate those who weren't. Many a man and woman threw themselves upon the weapons of the Patrol over personally meeting the Controllers' fierce capacity for mental warfare.

He tipped his hat at the questioning Patrol that hover near him. The people walked collectively toward their factory when they saw a strange pillar on the horizon, up near the hills that created the boundaries for the village. That pillar turned man, and the sun shadowed his features and dried the light sprinkle of rain droplets that had laid rested travel on his thin, ribbed body. He stared down the horizon upon the insignificantly-made people before him.

He tread downward, toward the cottage-laden town, feet heavily calloused from years of travel, and the tattered sandals he wore, with their make-shift straps that had long since snapped off. This stranger could see the smoky pillars of the Controllers far off into the edge of the world, but it lacked the proper intimidation for him.

At the bottom of the hill the people spoke in hushed tones, a stranger had never visited the lands before, especially not one clad in such attire, not one of such tones. Above his ratty sandals The Stranger had thoroughly faded, ripped, blue denim jeans. Above that was a tan vest that hung loosely from his shoulders, with small triangles acting as buttons undone. With his vest open like it was, the emaciated appearance of The Stranger became all the more well-known, skin looking as though it were squeezing him tight. Adorning The Stranger's head, hiding within his large, curly, black hair was a tightly wrapped red bandana. The bandana flowed beyond his hair, each tie glided lightly on the soft windfall that swiftly soared through this town so easily.

The people of the town backed up in fear of the two-headed man, but came to realize that his second head appeared a large case the color of his hair. He seemed barren of possession for all but the case and a strange gourd-like object wrapped in rags of varying colors, all on a spectrum of dirty grays and browns, which he held by a thin end. His face showed a feeling of deep thought soured with poor expectations as he moved around the crowd which seemed compelled to follow him, as though a pied-piper.

As he made way toward the blatant pub, a Patrol approached and requested identification. The Stranger proceeded past, while the Patrol hovered close. At another request, the rod was pulled and sparks crackled. The Patrol drew closer still, and as though without contemplation of consequence, The Stranger spun out of the path of the crackling rod, and at the apex of his

spin, he struck the Patrol with the broad side of his large gourd.
The Patrol fell, and the gourd made an unpleasant hum that
seemed to short out the rod. At the spin's climax, The Stranger
raised his ratty sandal skyward, dark oil stains gracing the
bottom, and brought it down with such force as to utterly
compress what would be the head of the Patrol. With a solid
crunch noise, like that of a crushed can, the Patrol whirred and
clicked, leaving only a soft beeping noise.

The people were shocked. A Patrol, an avatar of the
Controllers, so easily vanquished? And was that a smug smirk on
The Stranger's face? They now had little choice but to follow,
and so into the pub they all went as work was left undone.

The Stranger sat abruptly at a back table near a single
candle nearing its end, flickering quicker as the heat melted the
soft white wax. He took in the old décor and faint odors of
vanilla-smoke from the delicately crafted candle. He propped his
feet on the table and took off his sandals. As he did so, the
makeshift strap on one snapped. Disgruntled, The Stranger
tossed them aside, displaying thick soled heels to people of the
town who had flocked The Stranger.

He had shut his eyes momentarily after adjusting the case
on his back, and opened them with a bitter look in his face when
he saw all the people surrounding him. He kicked the table
several times. Shortly after, a small girl emerged from the crowd.

One of the few children in the town was an apprentice to
the pub, and she knew the signal as a desire to drink. She
brought a stout to The Stranger, who swallowed the frothy
mixture in two solid gulps. His eyes grew bigger as energy
seemed to restore him. His scratched his throat as though the
cold brew replenished his great thirst, and he signaled the lass for
another. Two more he drank, and when finished a large satisfied
sigh escaped his lips as he wiped his mouth with the rags of the
gourd. He seemed to be at peace now, and his bitter expression
turned a more tired one. Only then did the people of the town
start their rapid-fire questioning.

"What you did there sir, that was a ripe kind mistake it was!" Shouted one man.

"Right, but he did give the ol' Patrol a good whallop." One lady spoke with a satisfied nod.

"That may be, but now we're the ones getting the trouble for it," spoke a Frail Man at the back of the group. "They'll be sending more Patrol they will. Then work duty will double like last time."

The First Man spoke up louder, "Hey stranger! What's your name?"

The Stranger rocked back and forth in a state of slumber, his snore pouring from a drooling mouth.

"Wake up you! I'm asking something! Where you from?" The First Man shook The Stranger, but he simply collapsed against the man, deadweight in sleep.

"Looks like he is in pretty bad shape." Said the Lady of the Group as she tried to get him off the First Man. "Hey, there's something on this case. Looks like it says, 'Page Hendrix.' Think that's the poor sap's name?"

The Frail Man spoke up again, "I don't know and don't care. I say we all sit here to make sure he doesn't get away, and then turn him over to the Patrol. Let the Controllers deal with the miscreant. Me, I'm going to listen to muzak while I wait."

The people collectively seemed to jump back as The Stranger opened his eyes with their fierce, bitter look again. He looked out the window, and the people heard an old, but never forgotten sound; loud chirping gusts of wind. It meant only one thing, and The Stranger seemed to also be familiar with it. He touched the case on his back to make sure its location, and made haste to the door. His hand on the handle, the people rushed to hold him back.

"Ah let him go. Why bother now?" The Frail Man interrupted, as he turned up the worn-down radio's knobs. "We'll all get back to our normal work soon enough."

The Stranger broke free with a grumbled snort and turned to them tatters-worn gourd. They backed off and raised their arms for protection, but his gourd came down just the same. He gripped the handle to the pub and walked out smoothly. The people looked where his gourd fell to see their radio crushed the same as the previous Patrol, it winded down and became silent.

Nearby, rigid and white-faced, the Frail Man spoke, "Aaaaaah." He picked up the small radio pieces and they broke into even smaller pieces.

"We'll uh… We'll watch your shoes for you!" yelled the Lady of the Group to the door. The Little Pub Apprentice collected the flimsy, broken sandals and got to work mending with her nimble, dexterous fingers.

Outside The Stranger stood with the rags on his gourd flapping in the strong breeze pushing downward. Was the Patrol landing here, larger in number, with rods crackling in desired retribution, mounted shoulder weaponry glistened under an absent sun, cylindrical heads rising from within their bodies, for their destination was found. The Patrol landed and amassed with cunning advancement, slow and steady, like the endangered tiger.

The Stranger placed his hand hesitant upon the dark case on his back until reconsideration gripped him. With a head shake he removed his fingertips from the case and instead wrapped his hand in the rags loosely bound about the large gourd. He shook the gourd defensively at the Patrol who wavered not; they knew of The Stranger's methods from a final broadcast redly-beeped from the powered down remnants of their partner.

The Stranger jumped upward and thrust the narrow-end of the gourd into the cylindrical head of one Patrol. This Patrol sputtered and squealed away, the slowly blasted moments of electricity echoed upward through the body of the gourd, until the Patrol crashed to the ground with faded eyes.

The Stranger was one step to safety closer, but the Patrol could float metal encased wires, while he of spongy flesh was the servant of gravity. When The Stranger began descent, the Patrol rose to greet with an intense shock pushed deep into the soft tissue by many a rod.

The force of the electricity was of many volts unknown, but enough as to rocket The Stranger several yards away. His dark skin smoldered to a smoky texture which became an even darker shade, when gravity brought the man down once more.

The Patrol cared little for this and had their attention fixated on the gourd unraveled. In the resulted discipline of rods, the gourd had parted ways with The Stranger and freed from rags that encased it cocoon-like. The Patrol traced, with their sensors, a still attached piece of fabric tied toward the top-most narrow-end. They traced the dirty trail of discolored fabric all the way back to the hand of The Stranger, who held tightly on. A hand pushed up from the sandy, moist, muddy-colored cobblestone and The Stranger stood again. Injured, but standing.

Onyx eyes turned stone-like in indifference. The Stranger tugged. The cloth attached to the gourd pulled it upward and knocked two Patrol off-balance, landing upon their own rods, wiring rapidly malfunctioned as they bounced and rolled on the ground. As the gourd sailed in the air, the age of the rags finally gave way and split into eight separate pieces which glided to the ground. With a spring in his step, The Stranger met the gourd halfway and hugged it tightly to his chest.

Strings were pulled tightly across the front, one absent, and they grew tighter as The Stranger quickly adjusted the knobs on the narrow-end. The Stranger knew of the gourd as a guitar, specifically, a Fender Telecaster, its origins and design foreign to the land of this time. From faded leather he tore out a button, which The Stranger knew as a pick, and slammed his arm unto the strings. A terrible squeak poured out from the Telecaster which pushed the flailing Patrol on the ground up onto another pair of crackling rods from comrades behind. The next set of Patrol hovered defenseless, collectively. The whole legion knew what to do.

Their noisy engines roared; the blast of wind against the town's roads pushed away excess sand and fragile plant life. Soon even The Stranger's legs began to buckle under pressure exerted. He almost fell before readjusting the knobs once more.

He slammed his arms many a time over the strings and soon the pressure was at a standstill against the noise.

Inside the pub, the people still watched agape that one man could hold out against so many Patrol, which usually worked well enough alone to quell any town's riotous urges. But still the people sat pacified, because they knew what was coming. That and they all held their ears shut from the deafening leaf-blower noises of the Patrol on full force, and were in little condition to do much of anything. And yet there the Frail Man was determined to fix the antique radio, and the Little Pub Apprentice her mending.

The solid ballad of the Patrol against the screaming chords of The Stranger eventually held at middle-ground no longer, the tired noise giving way to the essence of variety. The spinning blades that kept the Patrol aloft soon whirred to a halt and grinded motors became all but glued into place. The Patrol soon resorted to walking legs designed upon spiders for ease of movement.

They clambered about the place, building windows covered in the sparkling metal carapaces of these robotic guards. It was a strategy planned out in circuitry for case of large rebellion. Though one man, surely he was of enough threat to execute the ideas of their masters. And so the Patrol were about The Stranger's arena, high and low, with mounted cannons opening, rods loosening to whips at full power.

This worried The Stranger not, for it had been some time since he had an audience to hear his tune. And so a supple melody poured out of his Telecaster. Though it had the occasional sharp note from strings in need of replacement, and a moment of silence from a string missed, it was pleasing to the ear, pleasing to the mind, but mostly, peaceful to the nature of things.

The Patrol shot their whips out and their mounted cannons shot harpoon-esque grappling ropes forward, magnetically attracted to iron-laden blood so common to humans. But soon offset were the weaponry of the Patrol, as the whips and

ropes seemed to rotate around The Stranger as he played his
melancholy song. As his voice cried out in hushed tones,
vibrations crawled up and along the various ropes and whips that
walled, circularly, The Stranger. These vibrations crept further
up the ropes and whips to make contact with the Patrol on the
ground and on the walls and on the rooftops.

Within time, the microcosmic vibrations had peeled into
every nook and cranny. They appeared to pause as though their
hollow bodies had felt pleasure for but a moment, before
programmed anger was quelled, and their construction willingly
fell apart, piece by tiny piece, until the Patrol had shed
themselves of everything.

The arena of The Stranger filled with audience no more;
now simply parts one to make a lawnmower, or maybe a lamp, or
possibly a fridge, or even a telescope. But The Stranger wasn't
interested in the constructs of mechanics, and so instead sat
cross-legged on the still moist cobblestone. He removed a pouch
from the faded leather vest's pocket. Out pulled a wrinkly sheet
of paper and poured a portion of the pouch's contents, dried
applewood tobacco, into the paper which he tightly rolled and
sealed with tongue's approval.

He also tore out a tiny, odd-looking, tan stick with a red
head, contained in a cover with worn-away words. He dragged
the head of the stick against a rough part of the Telecaster and
protected the resulted flame from wind's harm. A trail of smoke
punctured The Stranger's hand as the flame wove away. He
breathed deep and the tip of his rolled concoction glowed as
bright a red as any stick in his inventory.

The people in the pub piled out and stood in combined
interests. While some looked with bright eyes at this strange
scene with ears drenched in new sounds, others took on furrowed
brows and hand-covered mouths. The silence ended as a woman
from the crowd picked up a discarded piece of the Patrol. The
questions shot out almost as noisily as the guards who had only
recently held literal iron rule. Much like before, however, The
Stranger simply sat satisfied silently in his own vices, taking

short drag upon short drag until the red glowed so near his lips
that it burned his throat. It was then that he discarded the rolled
paper with a snap, where the smoke followed shortly behind.
The Little Pub Apprentice held the now mended sandals to The
Stranger who waved them off, he needed them not.

  The people of this little town became frustrated at The
Stranger's quiet, but failed to express it, for they were still
captivated by the wondrous new noises that flooded their roads
and seduced their ears. The cobblestone where The Stranger
played seemed stained, for their muddy colors changed from
black and gray to vibrant oranges and auburns.

  While the people of the town still pulled in close to The
Stranger, his heightened sense of hearing felt something of more
importance, and so took to his feet. Calloused soles acted just as
well as shoddy sandals. The gray storm advanced from the skies,
their tiny shapes from towers far away growing larger nearer the
town. The Stranger lifted his guitar once more and hugged it
tight. The people of the town crept slowly backward as the
snake-like fabrics of the Controllers charmed with fear.

  Much like The Stranger, they had nothing to say, the
evidence of their fallen mechanical avatars said it all. One from
the front of the crowd, who looked the same as every other
Controller, rose his hand in a peaceful manner and cracked a very
awkward smile that almost seemed to curl in on itself, truly a
frown trying to turn upside-down.

  The Stranger made no heed and raised his arm just the
same, pick in hand. As his arm came downward, the hand of the
front Controller turned and all the flesh on his face imploded to a
severely wrinkled raisin.

  A strong gust of wind made its way through the tight
road's corridors like a battering ram. The people, shaking as they
were, tried to hold back. They ended up soaring backward.
Some down narrower corridors, others crashed through windows
in tiny cottages, but just the same they all fell with brutal thuds.
The Stranger's legs buckled once more, but his main targets led
themselves before him, his only required audience, and his

fingers trembled throughout his body statuesque and remained solid on ground. A string from his guitar snapped and gouged deep into an onyx eye, and when a statue's structural point crumbles, so too does the remainder. The Stranger toppled over, yet managed to strike his Telecaster deep within the cobblestone, worn away from years unmanaged. The Stranger held tight, the wind tearing wider the gash near his mutilated eye. And like the roar of a leafblower, the solid noise of that gusting wind too died down. This left The Stranger still determined, sans one eye, but he needed vision not for his art.

As the wind halted The Stranger nearly stayed ignorant of the various wires and metal sheets building up around him. He had little time to deal with the magnum opus of Patrol made one, for he had his own stored away for this destined day. Before the machinery closed completely around The Stranger his nimble feet guided him through a crevasse almost large enough for him.

Almost large enough, for the leather vest and torn denim jeans became more so, their tough textures flayed. When The Stranger rolled, however, his only concern was to replace outdated clothing. An easier change than a new suit of skin. When feet met cobblestone again, he bounded from the roll to a skyward summersault.

Though blood washed his complexion, his aim was true and his summersault ended with but one gourd's last attempt, three strings not of much use to rock the granite hearts of the Controllers. The Telecaster extended outward and drew in near to the shoulder of the front Controller. His raisin-like face seemed to overlap even more wrinkles this time, and his spin seemed to crash into nothingness.

Whiplash almost weakened his grip, but instead dragged the Telecaster against the opposing force, where it began to squeal terribly off-key. The Controllers not in concentration cowered as one, while the front Controller held steady, deaf to the screeches even The Stranger could barely handle. Yet with one moment, The Stranger thought he saw into the front

Controller's soul, through his bloodshot mind's eye that ruptured under stress.

And so the Telecaster shattered the invisible barrier, wood splintered, the neck cracked, and the strings released their tension as the lightly rotted body broke into firewood. The Stranger likewise fell to ground with a popped thud, a dangerous sound for his shoulder.

All this happened not before the Telecaster cut its way deep into the body of the front Controller with violet blood squirting out in the consistency of curdled milk. Only when the front Controller was made two did the famed Telecaster join him.

The remaining Controllers and The Stranger, who was surprised his plan worked, moved not. Only when the nearly assembled mega-Patrol broke into mere fragments once more did action return. The Stranger's first move failed, his wounded shoulder gave out, and the Controller's picked up the pieces.

Their minds worked in tandem, a stronger wind, more adequately a hurricane, howled through the corridors, cobblestone uprooted, and nearby cottages caved in from the force. Paper-cuts formed from the piercing wind, made present over every exposed portion of The Stranger, who was pushed backward into the hill outside the town's boundaries.

The Controllers floated over to the hopeful stranger's grave, a perfect indentation of his body, like those old Roadrunner cartoons, where no movement or signs of breathing made themselves known. Content, the Controllers floated back to the town where aching people peaked from behind corners. Despite The Stranger's sole folly, the people too would be punished. And so the people of the town were made rag dolls, floating in the air via the Controllers' minds' eyes. They begged for mercy, which the Controllers took in like fine wine, the full flavor which had to be enjoyed before the people were crushed in a pitiful manner.

Wise as the Controllers were, they missed but one. One inspired enough to take matters to her own hands, and so the Little Pub Apprentice ran from hiding, and using only shoddy sandals as weapons, sang out an angry version of The Stranger's supple tune. The sandals, though soft, produced a meaningful slap-sounding beat. The Controllers switched their focus as one, and the people stuck in mid-air watched bone try to separate from the little girl. Despite best efforts, her angry song became a scared scream which echoed through the smashed corridors, which echoed through the skies and into the paths of passing birds, which echoed into perfectly shaped graves.

An earthquake shook the town, and the people fell from the Controllers' power. When those same torturers looked out beyond the town's boundaries, they saw soft soil erupted skyward, and above that soft, perfectly-orbed droplets of blood, but even higher still was the shadow of a villain most pertinent to the Controllers. He was opening that midnight-colored case on his back.

When this shadow landed, The Stranger had in his hands a shiny double-headed guitar, Gibson in nature, its specific style forgotten even to The Stranger. All this simple man knew, was that he held off on playing it until this moment, when it was needed most. The gleam from this black and blood-red guitar was so untouched, that it almost felt a shame for the natural oils of his hand to touch it. The knobs remained unadjusted, for it was perfectly tuned to the nature of things. Things so primitive it touched the very chromosomes within a strand of D.N.A. with but a single note.

The Stranger stood upon his two feet, his legs shook under the weight, but he would not sit for *his* magnum opus. His body was bruised, his body was bloody, but despite the paper-cuts which made his body look like a sheet of grid paper, despite his putrid pool of flesh in one eye socket, he still managed to strike fear into even the hearts of the Controllers with his cold stare. If their hearts were granite, he was the sledgehammer this world was missing, or rather, the stick of dynamite. His explosion would ring out over the lands.

The faces of all the Controllers turned raisin-like at once and not one, but two hands each rose. The force of the wind that rushed toward him tore through everything, almost sloughing aside reality, as streaks of purple rushed along the sides. It was the shape of a skyscraper-sized triangle, the strongest geometric shape.

The Stranger stood unafraid. He pulled a pick from a slot between the double-necks and made his arm the final tower the Controllers' power would need face. As the collective force dissolved everything before it, as it tore past the town's boundaries and into the hillside, The Stranger said the only thing outside song he ever would...

"Feel the power of my almighty axe!"

Suddenly The Stranger brought down his tower of an arm upon the first series of six strings, and then the next. It happened as the Controllers' collective power touched The Stranger. First his body seemed to blow apart, but as the sounds emerged from the guitar, his body collected itself, and the skyscraper-sized triangle toppled backward and shattered into trillions of pieces that disintegrated back to a harmless form of energy as it touched ground.

The sounds continued outward past the force and covered the town, and soon the entire countryside was stained in vibrant color. Dull brown grass grew lush and forest green. Trees likewise grew from wimpy saplings to something worthy of pride. The gray clothing on the people of the town fell apart, and under their scratchy cotton cloth were garments of varying colors and designs. The First Man had pictures of a record album on a t-shirt, the Frail Man wore a tight black leather jacket, and the Lady of the Group had a pretty Sunday dress on, the kind with sunflowers and a big billowing hat. The Little Pub Apprentice too went from simple attire to tie-dye and rocket shorts, a style popular only 150 years ago. The sandals she mended shrunk to fit her feet and were of fine material.

When the cottages were in complete repair with white and red roses hanging from windowsills, all of distinct creamy whites and oaken browns, with chimney red chimneys, the Controllers stood out like sore thumbs.

The Controllers gathered together as though one mass and tried their hands at turning the people against their savior. Their cowardly plans failed, however, as the people had a beat in their step, and a song on their breath. And so they hummed out the harmony as The Stranger's mellow voice started up a courageous melody. The Stranger became more like a close friend of bard-like qualities.

Faster and faster The Stranger attacked his own instrument as the tempo rose to incredible levels. 40 beats per minute, 50, 70, 110, 125, until finally it was of little use to count. Within moments, his fingers blistered and burst, bleeding ribbons wildly as he strummed away on his mighty axe with no intention of slowing.

The heavens themselves opened, and a mighty stairwell fell from the sky as the greats before him stood with their mighty guitars of choice; George Harrison, Keith Richards, Jimmy Hendrix, Chuck Berry, Jimmy Page, and countless others. A Woodstock attendance where only musicians need come.

Oh how glorious the sounds were that day as the people of the town stood in the roads, and the people of other villages far off heard the whispers of an artifact long since lost, music, and the power of rock.

The Controllers were forced back, the continuous flurry of flats and sharps too much for their oppressive ears. They used the parts of their dismantled Patrol as shields to warp themselves away at speeds faster than the music that played there, back to their Tower of Tyrants.

The people of the town were too captivated by the pleasure that tugged on the strings of their primitive D.N.A. to celebrate their retreat, and instead gathered before The Stranger as he played without heed, knowing not of their disappearance. His body glowed under mystical energies that the notes struck within his thin frame, and the ghosts of legends long past poured into the sweat and blood of The Stranger who erupted into a bright flash of nearly all colors be they red, blue, yellow, green, purple, azure, auburn, lapis, teal, magenta, or yet unnamed. This explosion rivaled even the fireworks put on by the people nearly 280 years ago.

When all was settled and the music rolled its final faded tune across the hillsides the country over, The Stranger, like the Controllers, was gone. But still the Controllers sat in their towers of technology supreme, planning. All that was left of The Stranger was a guitar, a simple one of cheap pine base, the gleaming double-neck no more. The people of the town stood stunned for a moment, and out from the crowd pushed a small girl, no longer attached to working the pub, wearing a tie-dye shirt, with durable, travel-ready sandals on foot.

She took up the guitar, which was much too big for her at the time, and pulled a string; a chord twanging abruptly outward. Needed practice, but seemed a good fit. She would grow into it.

As for The Stranger, the hero of the people, whatever happened to him? Was he but a simple spirit sent to release the people from dragged out oppression upon dulled people? Or was he really a man from mysterious places unknown? Would the gray Controllers with their obsessive bloodshot minds' eyes ever return? Surely they would, but now the people had hope, they had knowledge, and they were ready.

That Special Brand of Chinese

I done it. I finally done it. Stuck under the thumb of that bastard organization too long. Said the only way out is in a body bag, but I ain't the type to swallow a bullet, I'm a clean corpse that burns bright and is sore on the eyes like a fading horizon. No soiled rags for me. I stop off at the Chinese diner down the way. Nervously I peak through blinds closed over the window, make sure I'm not followed. Why would I?

"Hallo sah, may help you?" There stands a yellow man wearing all the proper waiter's attire, white shirt and black slacks. He holds a small board and smiles broadly with forced niceties.

"Yeah, get me an order of double-pork lo mein, one of them big cream-cheese wantons, and how about," I paused to peak out the window again, gotta be sure, "A plate of sweet-sour."

The Waiter nods and slides away. Almost forgot, "And a tub of scorched coffee, black as tar."

"No have coffee sah, only tea."

"Tea? Am I wearing a dress? What am I gonna do with stinkin' tea? You gonna bring it out here in a frilly tiki cup too, maybe throw in a wilting rosebud?" The Waiter folded his arms and pursed his lips tight. I wasn't really mad at ol' bowl-cut, "Listen pal, leaves is for giraffes. I may stick my neck out an awful lot, but... Just bring me a god damned cola, no ice. I hate having a loose grip."

Said the only way out is in a body bag, what a laugh. Took me years, long time to bring that plan together, to climb up the ladder to hear of the boss' whereabouts, much less see him. I used to think it was awful jokey to break Bruce Springsteen records. The dupes thought I didn't like catchy 80's rock, but I sure was dancin' in the dark when the plan pulled off.

Must have started about a year ago, just a small test. Made a drug sale, killed the dupes after the Fish left and then took a shot in the shoulder to pass it off. Told who I thought was boss the Fish pulled a fast one on us. Started a gang war, surf and turf, crackin' skulls. Those were the nights we called photo-shoots, because everywhere we went was a flash there, there, and there. Died down after a fake truce we betrayed the Fish on. Bad leadership, whole buncha goons floppin' out of the water. Numbers were too low to fight back, but the members ended up joining us at the Blue Dragons, because our flame was quenched, but our roar still clattered them boots.

They were a little suspicious of me when the Fish didn't take credit for the deal right away, but I did more jobs to cover my rap than a dog beggin' for scraps. Became a legend of a thug back then. Might as well have been a Fish, swimming in the trade as I did. A dragon kept its mouth out of water. Met the real boss and we hit it off big time. Making jokes about any ethnic group he wanted. Easy for me, didn't care so much for some of them anyway.

Took a huge job for boss, pulled it off easy. Was testing out a neat idea for my boys. They didn't have much kick, and the holster was always checked first. Kept a dud there. Got my idea from watching Taxi Driver. Guy was kinda messed up, but sure knew his firearms. Saved both my superiors' lives with the mock-up. Those dupes made a big noise about my marksmanship; made my personal caliber stronger than a desert eagle.

Remember Boss had said, *Thomas, ripening fruit of the Blue Dragons, you're goin' places.* Yeah, you too, and don't bother with a winter jacket. Wanted to see the thing I made too, wanted to know if I'd make him a copy for his collection. So I showed him, I showed his goons, and the dupes. They all got to see me flick my wrists. They all got to see the guns slide down. They all got to see what the front of a handgun looks like for a change.

"Food sah." The Waiter sets down the plates and cola, flat as Columbus' world. Chopsticks are placed on the table near me. The Waiter bows as he backs away.

"Wait a second, I'm not eating with no sticks. You bring me a fork and a knife. None of that standard placement crap either, hate holding forks in my *correct* hand." The Waiter comes back with haste and I set to fill my gullet with something other than satisfaction.

Took boss' solid silver gun. It never fired, and he only kept one bullet in the chamber, but I figured I would hold onto it if something went against the plan. Slipped the gun into the holster underneath the right flap of my jacket, easier to shoot left-handed I always thought. Why be right when I can be sinister? I figured long as I was there I'd switch the jacket of my suit with one of the goons my size too. Those sliding mounts on my forearm forced me to wear a baggy suit, made me look like a slob and a damn kid when my hands kept slipping into the sleeves. One look at my paint job and decided to leave 'em as they were. What a mess.

There weren't many loyal Blue Dragons left, most never heard of me, most didn't care. Those that did found me before I ever left the building. I don't quite remember everything that happened; all I know is that I'm the last Blue Dragon. I was the last Blue Dragon. Now I'm a phoenix getting my life back through the fire. Too bad though, because I'm still looking down my suit sleeve and seeing that length of dragon tattoo with the blue ink on the bottom of my arm. I'm not the phoenix.

I munch my teeth through the tough chicken and that tangy sauce tingling my tongue as I wipe my mouth clean. I peak out through those blinds again. No new cars, good. I hear a brief clack to my other side and I feel the silver burning through my chest. I reach into the right pocket.

Damned Chinaman scares the wits out of me, laying that bill down. Bill? Plates are clean, guess I don't know how fast I'm eating, but the Waiter sure does pay attention. He was gone and a fortune cookie took his place. I really wish they'd keep these things in their plastic wrappers. Guess they must think its some sort of service to unwrap them for the customers, getting their grubby hands all over them. Explains the price. Who knows how often they wash. I hear a crack from the cookie, but it feels really stale. God I wish they kept them in a wrapper, instead of throwing them in a box with the rest of them. Old bird food.

I toss a piece of the cookie in my mouth and munch, so damn chewy. Gotta make it through, can't read the fortune for a cookie I haven't eaten. Tastes awful funny though, not even like an old cookie, more like, well, I can't quite place it. Not much like a cookie, damn sure of that.

Ah whatever. I'd have to remember to buy a cheese grater and some iodine before I left the state. I can just bite down on my belt, its tough enough.

This cookie is terrible, what a bitter taste in my mouth, the fortune better be worth it. No wonder this place is empty, probably have health code violations up the wing-wang. Ha, wing-wang ching-chang. Still, food has that charm to it, like something long ago. I don't know, I'm just trying to rid myself of this flavor by sipping down the last of my cola, warm and stale.

I reach for that little scrap of paper in the cookie, and learn another word of Chinese. What a coincidence, blue: lanse. Who gives a shit about the lucky numbers, I need that insight into the philosopher behind this operation. Probably some yellow-man behind a lever he pulls all day as the press comes down. What a laugh.

Wait a minute, out of state? That's right! I can go anywhere I want now. I could take a piss in Michigan and grab a drink down in Ohio if I want. All I have to worry about is not to speed, keep track of my dead-weight foot. Seems like a small worry compared to not having cold metal squeezed against my temples all the time.

It's damn hot in here. Wish they'd turn on the central, beginning to feel sick. Here's the Waiter, gotta tell him to turn the... My fortune, gotta read that. *Many a false step has been made standing still*? What's that s'posed to mean?

"Waiter, waiter," I tug at my tie, "Is there air in here? Turn it up, way up. It's suddenly so hot."

"No cool air here, sah." The Waiter wipes his brow with an apron.

"Look at ya, you're sweating away too, all greasy and wet. But you don't look sick, you must be used to this humid weather huh? No, that ain't it. You look more like you're nervous, expecting. Damn it's hot. Feel like I'm gonna pass out. Get that lousy cook, food's bad, real bad."

"Cook gone today, sah."

"So what, you the cook today? You wash them grubby hands before touching my food? You're making me sick, this place is spinning like a screwy carousel. Get me a glass of ice, a bucket." Gotta loosen my tie, but its so tight, I can't do it. Feel like I'm choking, being hung while sitting. Buy some of those stomach pills on the way out of state.

"Sah, have you ever hear story of man try to clean beach?"

"Cleaning a beach? What are you on about?"

"Man try to clean beach by grabbing up every grain of sand, but beach large and sand small, so man always miss one." The Waiter says this as he begins to roll one sleeve to the upper arm, the other arm rolling up the other. I see an interesting design, a rather intricate dragon under the forearm, with a twinge of blue. Looks like it's on top of a pair of gills and a tail-fin.

"Fuck. The fortune cookie, you sonnafabitch. Tasted like bad dishsoap, you yellow-bellied squint." Never thought of keeping an eye on the kitchen rather than the parking lot.

Suddenly that silver gun is the heaviest thing in the world, and it almost pulls me down to Hell itself. But I ain't goin' down like that, all works out to karma. Boss got his, I get mine, yeller over here will too. I reach into my left inner-jacket pocket.

The Waiter takes a step back with a woodsman's stance, pulling out a large rectangular blade, straight from the chopping block. Duck's neck now mine. His determination seems to trail up the length of the blade as the weak fluorescent lighting glows on its edge. It takes some effort, weak, heaving, and moist as I am, but I get my hands around what I'm looking for.

"Always another one from the fire, no matter how hot," because I know there's no fire without a spark. My arm manages to flop onto the table, the rest of me with it, this chiseled mug squishing down into a ceramic plate still soiled with sweet and sour sauce. My hand crumples open and wrinkly dollar bills pop out on top of the bill. "Here's a tip, I'm left-handed asshole."

Made in the USA
Monee, IL
11 August 2022

11371236R10111